Call For The Intercessors

Sound The Alarm
It's Mourning Time

Prayer Anthology Vol. I

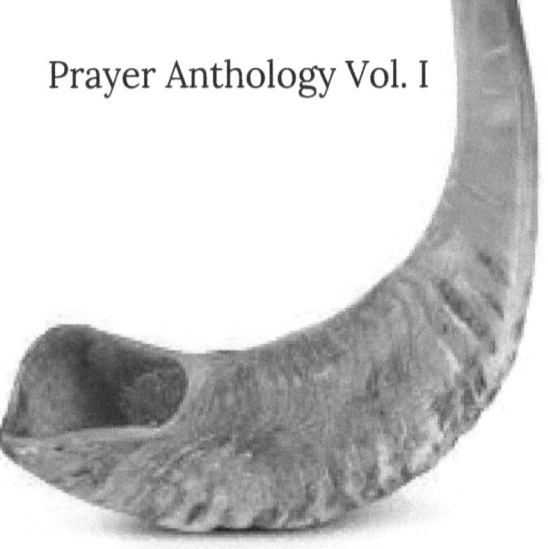

Tammy M. Isaac, DMIN
Editor and Co-Author

Call for The Intercessors: Sound the Alarm, It's Mourning Time

Copyright © 2025 by Tammy M. Isaac

Copies of this book are available at quantity discounts for bulk purchases.

For more information, contact:
Dr. Tammy M. Isaac
www.drtammyisaac.com
Email: tammymisaac@aol.com

Unless otherwise noted,

Used by permission. All rights reserved.

ISBN: 979-8-9914943-4-2

Printed in the United States of America. All rights reserved. No part of this book may be reproduced or transmitted in any form or by any means, electronic or mechanical, including photocopying, recording, or any information storage and retrieval system, without written permission of the publisher except for brief quotations used in reviews, written specifically for inclusion in newspapers, blogs, or magazines.

Cover Design: Candice Kilgore, Think. Create. Build.

Book Production: Tammy M. Isaac, Nema Grace Media Group

Call For The Intercessors

Sound The Alarm
It's Mourning Time

Prayer Anthology Vol. I

Blow the trumpet in Zion; sound the alarm on my holy hill" (Joel 2:1, NIV).

DEDICATION

To the People of God,

This work is for you—the faithful, the weary, the hopeful, and the broken. To every intercessor who has quietly stood in the gap, to those who have prayed in the midnight hour when no one saw, and to those who have wept for families, churches, and nations: this is your clarion call.

May this book strengthen your resolve, ignite your spirit, and deepen your commitment to prayer. You are God's chosen vessels—His watchmen on the walls, His wailing women, and His prophetic voices. Your prayers matter. Your obedience shifts the heavens.

This is dedicated to all who have heard the call and all who will answer. May you continue to seek Him, hear Him, and move mountains through your faith.

With love, faith, and reverence,

The Co-Authors

TABLE OF CONTENTS

PREFACE vii
INTRODUCTION vii
CALL FOR THE IMPRECATORY PRAYER WARRIOR 1
CALL FOR THE LEADERSHIP INTERCESSOR 49
CALL FOR THE FASTING PRAYER 70
CALL FOR THE WAILING WOMEN 119
CALL FOR THE ELDERS 169
CALL FOR THE INTERCESSORS 202
CALL FOR THE PRAYING MOTHER 229
CALL FOR THE PROPHETIC INTERCESSOR 256

PREFACE

We are living in critical and uncertain times—spiritually, socially, and globally. The world is groaning under the weight of conflict, chaos, and brokenness. The foundations of families, churches, and communities are being shaken, and many are searching for hope, healing, and restoration. In moments like these, God raises up a remnant: intercessors—those who stand in the gap, cry out for mercy, and seek heaven's intervention on behalf of others.

This anthology is more than a collection of words; it is a clarion call—a trumpet sounding in the spirit realm, urging believers to rise and take their place on the frontlines of prayer. As the prophet Joel declares, "*Blow the trumpet in Zion; sound the alarm on my holy hill*" (Joel 2:1, NIV). Now, more than ever, we must awaken to the urgency of the hour, stepping

Preface

into our role as intercessors and prayer warriors, with hearts fully surrendered to God.

Call for the Intercessors: Sound the Alarm, It's Mourning Time is a sacred work, born out of obedience and a deep awareness of the season we are in. The authors in this anthology—each anointed and experienced in the ministry of intercession—have answered the call to share their insights, testimonies, and strategies for powerful, effective prayer. Through their words, you will find wisdom, encouragement, and practical tools to help you navigate the journey of intercession.

Each chapter reflects a unique dimension of prayer, drawing from biblical principles and personal experiences. From the wailing women and prophetic intercessors to the prayer warriors and fasting leaders, this book brings together voices that echo one powerful

Preface

truth: prayer changes things. Intercessors are not bystanders; they are spiritual gatekeepers, charged with pulling down strongholds, standing in the gap, and declaring the will of God over people, communities, and nations.

This is not a time for complacency. It is a time to sound the alarm. It is mourning time—a season to repent, seek God's face, and cry out for deliverance and restoration. The call is urgent, and the time is now. This book is a guide, a resource, and a rallying cry for every believer who feels the weight of intercession and desires to be used by God for such a time as this.

As you turn these pages, let the Holy Spirit stir your heart. Allow the words to challenge and inspire you. Commit to becoming the intercessor God is calling you to be. Together, we will rise, stand in the gap, and pray until we

Preface

see heaven move and God's glory revealed on earth. The call has been issued. Will you answer it?

Dr. Tammy Isaac, DMin
Editor and Co-Author

INTRODUCTION

It is the duty of the watchmen on the walls to sound the shofar, to warn of danger, and impending destruction, and when there is found a breach in the wall of the city. Likewise, in the church the alarm is to be sounded when the ordinances, the statutes, the judgments, the precepts, and the counsels have been breached! Breach is to break or act contrary to (a law, promise, etc.).

The shofar horn is one of the most powerful and symbolic instruments found in scripture. Its sound is not merely noise—it is a divine alarm that calls God's people to attention, repentance, and action. Historically, the shofar was blown to signal times of war, spiritual awakening, mourning, and renewal. Its echoes reverberate through the pages of the Bible as a reminder of God's call to His people to return to Him, stand firm, and pray without ceasing.

Introduction

In ancient Israel, the shofar was used to gather God's people and prepare them for what lay ahead. Whether it was an impending battle, a time of repentance, or a moment to celebrate the start of a new season, the blast of the shofar served as a call to action. In the Book of Joel, the Lord commands, *"Blow the trumpet in Zion; sound the alarm on my holy hill"* (Joel 2:1). The sound of the shofar was a warning and a plea for the people to repent, pray, and prepare. This same urgency lies at the heart of *Call for the Intercessors: Sound the Alarm, It's Mourning Time*.

The shofar's blast also signaled spiritual warfare. When Joshua led the Israelites around the walls of Jericho, the blowing of the shofar was an act of obedience and faith that brought the walls crashing down (Joshua 6:1-20). It was not the sound of the horn itself, but the power of God working through His obedient people in response to their prayers.

Introduction

Today, intercessors are called to this same spiritual battle. Through prayer and fasting, they tear down strongholds, break chains, and open the way for God's deliverance and restoration.

Furthermore, the shofar carries a connection to mourning and repentance. During the Jewish High Holy Days of Rosh Hashanah and Yom Kippur, the shofar is blown to signal self-reflection, humility, and a return to God. Mourning in the biblical sense is not only about grief but also about turning our hearts back to God, seeking forgiveness, and aligning ourselves with His will. As intercessors, we are called to take on this mantle of mourning, crying out to God on behalf of those who are hurting, broken, and in need of His divine intervention.

The significance of the shofar is woven throughout the themes of this anthology. Like

Introduction

the shofar's blast, this book is a call for believers to rise up, awaken to the urgency of the times, and engage in deep, intentional prayer. It is a cry for intercessors to stand in the gap for individuals, families, communities, and nations. Each chapter serves as a distinct "blast," resonating with its own unique tone and message, but all sounding the same call: it's time to pray, repent, and seek God with all of our hearts.

This is not a passive call. It is a clarion call to action. The authors of this anthology, each in their unique anointing, have written to encourage, equip, and inspire you. You will find wisdom, testimonies, and practical guidance to deepen your role as an intercessor. You will be challenged to step into spiritual warfare, embrace seasons of mourning and fasting, and pray with the boldness and authority that God has given His people.

Introduction

As you begin this journey, allow the words of this book to stir your spirit. Let the shofar's symbolic sound echo in your heart. The time for complacency is over. The walls must come down. The nations must be covered in prayer. The hurting must be lifted before the throne of grace.

Sound the alarm. It's mourning time.

Dr. Tammy Isaac, DMin
Editor and Co-Author

The sound of the shofar is not just a call to action; it is a cry from the depths of the spirit, summoning God's people to awaken, repent, and intercede. In times of mourning, it reminds us that through prayer and faith, we partner with heaven to bring forth renewal and restoration.

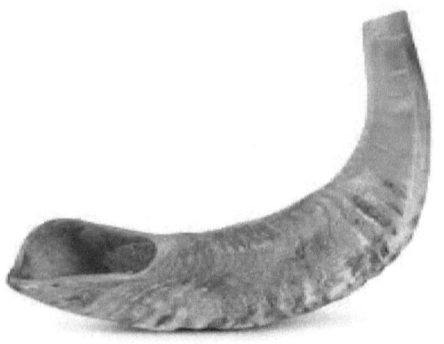

1

CALL FOR THE IMPRECATORY PRAYER WARRIOR

Dr. Brenda Arnold-Scott

King David must have been severely, emotionally wounded when he prayed, "May his children be fatherless and his wife a widow."[1] In times of unexpected, severe emotional pain, one can find oneself standing

---

[1] Psalm 109:9 (NIV).

Call for The Imprecatory Prayer Warrior

in the space of perceived obscenity. Many have perished there. But David was at his wit's end and needed a wits-end resolution. Israel appears similarly affected when it prays by the rivers of Babylon that God allows it to forget its inherent hymnody gifts and expresses profound happiness at the thought of Babylonian children being dashed against rocks. While others have written these prayers, David is credited as the author of many of them. Even with his great love for God, David thought it not robbery to unleash such lexical assaults where he petitions God to break the teeth out of the enemy's mouth.[2] Reed Lessing, who shares the thoughts of a broad theological community, ponders the question, "How did such barbaric words make their way into the prayer book of God's people."[3] He believes that such text does not

---

[2] Psalm 58:6 (NIV).
[3] Reed Lessing. ""Broken Teeth, Bloody Baths, and Baby Bashing: Is There Any Place in the Church for Imprecatory Psalms?"." *Concordia Journal 32, No.4*, October 2006: 368.

Call for The Imprecatory Prayer Warrior

appear to be a part of the traditions taught by Matthew to love one's enemies, turn the other cheek, walk the extra mile, bless, and do not curse.[4]

J. Carl Laney addresses the problematic nature of these Psalms for Bible teachers and preachers because of the difficulty in reconciling them with Christian thought.[5] This resistance by faith communities to teach, discuss, and generally include these kinds of prayers as part of the spiritual program of the church, robs the Body of Christ of a particular healing thread that comes only through these words. These prayers, primarily found in the Book of the Psalter (Psalms), cover every human emotion. They envelop both extremes of the pendulum, taking one from orientation to disorientation to new orientation. For the

---

[4] Matthew 5:38-44 (KJV).
[5] J. Carl Laney, "A Fresh Look at the Imprecatory Psalms" *Bibliotheca Sacra* 138, no. 549 (January – May 1980): 35.

Call for The Imprecatory Prayer Warrior

Body of Christ to experience the fuller dimensions of healing that come through the reflective meditational nature of the imprecatory psalms; the community of faith must reconcile these psalms with Christian thought. Moreover, believers, too, must seek the way of reconciling them, for the effort of seeking, is enriching. There is so much that transcends from seeking communion with God, learning to abide, and ultimately, finding God at the point of one's most profound need.

When the Israelites were exiled to Babylon, the experience was so traumatic that it disrupted Israel's mind to praise God. Instead, Israel weeps in righteous indignation and declares that it can neither sing nor play Zion songs again. Herein, pain reduces Israel to a state of barrenness. This barrenness is idiomatic of the posture that the church has taken with imprecation psalms. For the church to access its healing, it must access

Call for The Imprecatory Prayer Warrior

these psalms as freely as it accesses the non-controversial scriptures. The Book of Psalms is written in the language of God, and what better way to communicate with anyone, including God, than in His own language, even if it is the language of imprecation. Pitts cites Brueggemann's point that if you engage with people, life is life under assault, from which he deduces that vengeance is simply an insistence for God to do justice. Further, Pitts asks, "What shall we do with the vengeance we feel? He concludes, "We act it out, deny it, or put it on God's desk."[6] The purpose of this chapter is to bring a little-known or an unknown subject matter from behind the walls of teaching institutions and scholarly debate and discussion, into a world that needs this living, healing bread; and to present perspectives on why and how to pray imprecatory prayers. Further, the hope is to

---

[6] From OT 721 Lectures by Dr. Charles Pitts, Ph.D., Thursday March 5, 20009.

Call for The Imprecatory Prayer Warrior

encourage faith communities to teach reconciliation of these imprecation psalms with Christian thought; and incorporate them in their spiritual programs.

IMPRECATION PSALMS

Laney describes imprecation as an invocation of judgment, calamity, or curse uttered against one's enemies or enemies of God.[7] He points to Moses' prayer in Numbers 10:35, where Moses prays for God's enemies, who were his enemies, to be scattered; and to flee from his presence. Another example of imprecatory presence is found in Acts 13:11, where Paul curses a sorcerer, and induces him to a blind state. Not only are imprecations included in scripture other than the Psalms, but they are also prevalent in both the Old Testament and New Testament. Laney

---

[7]Laney, 36.

Call for The Imprecatory Prayer Warrior

believes that crucial to the definition of imprecation is its invocatory nature as a prayer or request to God that one's enemies or God's enemies be judged and justly punished.[8] Leupold states that imprecatory psalms are psalms in which the writer prays that God afflicts evildoers and punishes them according to his just deserts.[9] Harrison remarks that these psalms are a reply to national enemies, and a call to God to exercise retribution.[10] Thus, the passion of imprecations is a cry for justice, not vengeance or vindictiveness. It is a cry for help in times of trouble. It is the desperate cries of one experiencing the absence of God, but who longs for His help.

John Day describes imprecations as the troublesome portion of the Scriptures that

---

[8] Laney, 36.
[9] H. C. Leupold, The Psalms (Grand Rapids Baker Book House, 1969) p 18.
[10] Ronald K. Harrison, *Introduction to the Old Testament* (Grand Rapids Wm. B. Eerdmans Publishing Co., 1969), p 997.

Call for The Imprecatory Prayer Warrior

express the desire for God's vengeance to fall on His enemies and include the use of actual curses or imprecations.[11] A prevailing school of thought encourages fear of the imprecatory psalms and other imprecations in the Bible by pointing at the characteristic of the psalm that incorporates the dreaded curse. This concept seems to reach around the holy nature of God and places His Word and the power that is intrinsic to His Word, in the same category as acts of divination, sorcery, and voodoo. Through the annals of time, *God has shown Himself strong on behalf of those whose hearts are loyal to His (2Ch 16:9 NKJV)*. Thus, His justice, which at times comes out of His wrath and anger, is fair.

What are these imprecatory psalms? Bratcher lists seven of them—*Psalm 35, Psalm 69, Psalm 83, Psalm 88, Psalm 109, Psalm 137,* and *Psalm*

---

[11] John N. Day, "The Imprecatory Psalms, and Christian Ethics." *Bibliotheca Sacra* 159, no. 634 (April–June 2002): 166-186.

Call for The Imprecatory Prayer Warrior

140.[12] In *Psalm* 35, David asks for vindication. In *Psalm* 69, David pours out his grief and asks for God's anger upon his enemies. *Psalm* 88 is a cry for help. David speaks only of his plight in this psalm. In *Psalm* 109, David pleads for his accusers to be clothed with shame. In *Psalm* 137, Israel prays for the day God executes the same destruction and vengeance upon Babylon that it has executed upon The Holy City Jerusalem. In *Psalm* 140, David prays for deliverance from the wicked. The imprecatory psalm is a specialized type of lament psalm. Like the imprecatory psalm, the lament also includes a cry for help. Out of the 150 psalms, DeClaisse´-Walford classifies 67 of them as lament psalms. They are 3, 4, 5, 6, 7, 9, 10, 11, 12, 13, 14, 15, 16, 17, 22, 25, 26, 27, 28, 31, 35, 36, 38, 39, 40, 42, 43, 51, 52, 53, 54, 55, 56, 57, 58, 59, 60, 61, 62, 63, 64, 69, 70, 71, 74, 77, 79, 80, 83, 85, 86, 88, 90, 94, 102, 106, 108, 109, 120, 123, 126, 130,

---

[12] Dennis Bratcher, List of "Types of Psalms: Classifying the Psalms by Genre" provided by Dr. Chuck Pitts in OT 721 Class.

Call for The Imprecatory Prayer Warrior

137, 140, 141, 142, and 143.[13] Lessing categorizes the imprecatory psalms into three groups: imprecations against societal enemies (58, 94) national enemies (68, 74, 79, 83, 129, 37), and personal enemies (5, 6, 7, 9, 10, 17, 28, 31, 35, 40, 52, 54, 55, 56, 59, 69, 70, 71, 104, 109, 139, 140, 141, 143).[14] According to Edismore, *Psalms* 7, 35, 55, 58, 59, 69, 79, 109, 137, and 139 all contain imprecations pleading for God's judgment upon one's enemies.[15] According to Fretheim, "Prophetic literature is filled with violent speech and action, both human and divine. He concludes that there would be no divine violence without human violence. *Lamentations* 2:19-21 notes God's judgment on women, children, and the environment. Fretheim points out that this kind of violence

---

[13] Nancy L. DeClaisse´-Walford, An Introduction to the Psalms: A Song from Ancient Israel, (St. Louis: Chalice Press, 2004), 145-150.
[14] Lessing, 368.
[15] John Eidsmoe, "Imprecation? Biblical? Christian?" *Christianity, Law, Miscellaneous, Morality, Speech, Uncategorized, Firm Foundation,* Official Blog of the Foundation of Moral Law at http://morallaw.org/blog (accessed May 9, 2009).

Call for The Imprecatory Prayer Warrior

disturbs Christian thought and is considered troubling to theologians."[16] Imprecatory theology is found in other Old Testament scriptures, such as *Genesis 18, Exodus 32, Habakkuk 1,* and *Jeremiah 27.* New Testament imprecations include *Matthew 11, Acts 8, Galatians 5,* and *Mark 11.*

The movement of imprecation typically weaves a brief prayer between the revelations of one's problem and the reality of God's absence in one's deliverance. According to McCann, the basic movement of the psalm, the literary style under which the imprecation falls, begins with (1) a vocative and continues with a description of the trouble, (2) protests of God's wrath, (3) pleas for relief, (4) affirms trust in God, and (5) offers a promise to praise.[17] These five movements are typical of the lament psalm but may or may not be

---

[16] Terrence E. Fretheim, "I Was a Little Angry: Divine Violence in the Prophets." *Interpretation* 50, no. 4 (October 2004): 62.
[17] J. Clinton McCann, Jr., "Psalms," 44.

Call for The Imprecatory Prayer Warrior

included in an imprecation. An imprecatory example is *Psalm 88*. Seven movements in this psalm contain three of the five essential elements of the lament psalm. The movements consist of prayer, a portrait of the psalmist's pain, and protests between pleas to God. Although the psalmist cries out to God and speaks of God's attributes, such as His righteousness, he does not affirm his hope and trust by praising God beyond this acknowledgment. He begins the psalm in a disoriented state and ends similarly. There is no resolution for the psalmist. Generally, there is a profession of confidence in the lament psalms. There is no distinct profession of the faith or trust of the psalmist in this psalm other than his cry to the LORD, God of his salvation.

There are three references to prayer or the psalmist's reminder to God that he has already prayed. The absence of God propels the psalmist to a heightened state of despair, as evidenced by the use of such words as cry, troubles, pit, afflicted, heavy, dark, distraught, destructive, dead, grave, wrath, etc. As this psalmist uses both synonymous and synthetic parallelism to describe his pain in Psalm 88, these literary features are standard to the imprecatory nature of psalms.

EARLY TWENTY-FIRST CENTURY THEORETICAL DISCUSSIONS

Gaiser takes a radical position against the teaching and sharing of imprecation prayers in the Christian faith. He argues:

> "Still, we can't allow them, can't we? Once God has taken God's wrath upon himself in Jesus Christ, how can we call down God's wrath on others? Once Jesus has asked God to forgive his murderers, how can we not even forgive the terrorists among us? Once we have heard Jesus' radicalization of the law, how can we divide between

Call for The Imprecatory Prayer Warrior

> them and us, as only "they" are wicked? The danger is more apparent when we recognize that in the present international crisis, "they" are praying with equal fervor against us and often using the same psalms.[18]"

Gaiser believes one prays against oneself when one prays for one's enemy, therefore, the imprecatory psalms are dangerous. Robert Thomas argues that a rarely discussed, prominent source of God's eschatological wrath is the vindictive toned prayers of the saints.[19] Gerald Pauls adds that there is a deep resistance toward allowing the emotions of bitter hatred and vengeance to be considered a legitimate expression of the Christian faith.[20] Finally, Gary Anderson shares that the imprecatory psalms are no longer required reading for priests and monastics who, in

---

[18]Frederick J. Gaiser, "Deliver Us from Evil," *Word & World* 22 No. 1 (Winter 2002): 3.

[19] Robert L. Thomas, "Imprecatory Prayers of the Apocalypse," *Bibliotheca Sacra* 126 no. 502.

[20] Gerald Pauls, "The Imprecations of the Psalmists: A Study of Psalm 54," Direction Home Page, 1993 Direction, at http://www.directionjournal.org /article/ 806 (accessed May 6, 2009).

their respective offices, are charged with daily prayer because as concerns the practice of religious life, they have been removed from the record.[21]

Proponents of imprecation would hold that while these views may be convincing, they do not reflect a healthy approach to the Book of Psalms. Although Pauls makes a statement of fact concerning the pervasive negative attitudes about teaching imprecation psalms, he also believes the tension between "loving" and "cursing" can be harmonized, that Christians must continually seek reconciliation, practice longsuffering, forgiveness, and kindness, that times come when justice must be enacted, whether directly from God or through His representatives (in particular the state and judicial system *Rom* 13:1-4).[22] Another

---

[21] Gary A. Anderson, "King David and the Psalms of Imprecation," *Pro Ecclesia* 15, no. 3 (Summer 2006): 267-280.
[22] Pauls, 83.

proponent of the imprecation, Lessing takes a bold stand and asserts that pastors who minister to those facing sustained injustice, hardened enmity, and gross oppression must teach the baptized to pray imprecatory psalms. He is persuaded that these psalms are God's gift so that sufferers are able to hold fast to their human dignity while at the same time enduring hardship nonviolently.[23] Luther supports Lessing's theory and boldly proclaims that one should pray for enemy's conversion to one's friend; if not, one's doing and designing are bound to fail and have no success, and that one's person perishes rather than the Gospel and the kingdom of Christ."[24] For this research the views examined were one on one—one proponent of imprecation for every opponent. If one is undecided at this point as to whether imprecations should or

---

[23] Lessing, 369-370.
[24] Luther's Works, vol.21, The Sermon on the Mount and the Magnificat, eds. Jaroslav Pelikan and A.T.W. Steinhauser (St. Louis: Concordia, 1956), 1000).

Call for The Imprecatory Prayer Warrior

should not be taught, shared, preached, and prayed; Lessing's final argument may leave one deciding in favor of them. In this discussion of pros and cons, Lessing concludes:

> A war is transpiring, a war of opposing powers with eternal consequences. In this war, the baptized experiences casualties, traitors, and triumphs. Our weapon is the sword of the Spirit, with the Word of God (Eph 6:17). This weapon includes both the kindness and the severity of God (Rom 11:22). In times of acute and ongoing distress, we must invoke the severity of God as expressed in the imprecatory psalms. It is our way of coming before the Lord and throwing the sword to Him, for "the battle belongs to the LORD (1Sam 17:47).[25]

---

[25] Lessing, 370.

Call for The Imprecatory Prayer Warrior

TWENTY-FIRST CENTURY VOICES

I engaged this study in response to an Old Testament assignment as a student working toward my Master of Divinity. We received a list of topics from which to choose. "Imprecations in Theology," were among those topics. I was unfamiliar with imprecation theology, but I always strive to add knowledge, and not just rewarm or repeatedly reconstruct the same theories. I can further elucidate and admit; that in terms of my prayer life; I was really tired of praying the same prayers, and not experiencing a move of God. Thus, I desired to gain a deeper and more profound understanding of the breadth and depth of the Word of God, for such understanding is the wellspring of life. As I engaged in deep study, I was surprised to learn that God had already carried me through an imprecatory experience; but

Call for The Imprecatory Prayer Warrior

because I was unaware and untaught, I did not have any information to consider this weapon in the Word of God. As a student of theology or the study of God; it was an honor and privilege to attend seminary where I studied and learned at the highest levels. I am always seeking opportunities to pay it forward. Thus, one of my goals is share these gems with others. Herein, I hope to accomplish that in this chapter—to teach you, the reader, what I have both learned and benefitted from.

I began studying this subject matter in the early 2000s, two decades ago. Thus, herein presented are current trends and views of imprecation proponents. On such current day theologian is Charles B. Wagner who defends the imprecatory psalms, asserting that in Psalm 57, "the destruction of man qua man is not celebrated, only the destruction and judgment of man God is celebrated, for God hath no pleasure the destruction of the living.

Call for The Imprecatory Prayer Warrior

Instead, the object of His rejoicing is in expressing His justice, for the LORD loveth justice."[26]

Further, Wagner deduces a lengthy conclusion that this writer believes is apropos. Thus, the entire narrative is cited to put teeth into supporting the theory that all God-breathed Scriptures have been given to as a collection of swords to wield during drastic trials, so that one might be sufficiently dressed to win! He writes:

> In conclusion, as we have seen, there is no reason to remove the imprecatory psalms from the church's liturgy. Instead, we ought to follow St. Augustine's advice in De Doctrine Christiana; if the sentence is one of command, either forbidding a crime or vice, or enjoining an act of prudence or benevolence, it is not figurative. If, however, it seems to enjoin a crime or vice or forbid an act of prudence or

---

[26] Wagner, Christian B., Scholastic Answers A Defense of the Imprecatory Psalms (christianbwagner.com).

benevolence, it is figurative. Scripture says: If your enemy hungers, feed him; if he thirsts, give him a drink; this is beyond doubt a command to do kindness. But in what follows, for in so doing you shall heap coals of fire on his head, one would think a deed of malevolence was enjoined. Do not doubt, then, that the expression is figurative. While it is possible to interpret it in two ways, one pointing to the doing of an injury, the other to a display of superiority, let charity, on the contrary, call you back to benevolence and interpret the coals of fire as the burning groans of penitence by which a man's pride is cured who bewails that he has been the enemy of one who came to his assistance in distress. In the same way, when our Lord says, He who loves his life shall lose it, we are not to think that He forbids the prudence with which it is a man's duty to care for his life, but that He says in a figurative sense, let him lose his life — that is, let him destroy and lose that perverted and unnatural use which he now makes of his life, and through which his desires are fixed on temporal things so that he gives no heed to eternal. It is written: Give to the godly man and help not a sinner. The latter clause of this sentence seems to forbid benevolence, for it says, help not a sinner. Understand, therefore, that sinner is put figuratively for sin so that it is his sin you are not to help.[27]

I encourage every reader to allow your learning, seeking, and studying to be informed by God, through the Holy Spirit, who guides us, illuminates our minds, and teaches us all things. Remember, these imprecatory prayers are designed to win the war. *In the beginning was the Word and the Word was with God, and the Word was God (John 1:1).* This Word is God. Thus, God is fighting one's battles and winning one's wars when one speaks His Word. When One gives God His Word, it shall not return void. Believe it!

Thus, we look at another 2023-2024 proponent of imprecation, Liz Cooledge Jenkins, as she reflects on national disturbia

---
[27] Wagner

Call for The Imprecatory Prayer Warrior

and righteous indignation over current events, particularly as death and cornage invade Ukraine. She also looks to stalwart Walter Bruggemann to help societies process the spills of a war being waged today. Cooledge recalls the agony expressed by those who question why God is allowing children and the vulnerable to experience such violence. Then she recalls Bruggemann's perspective that imprecatory psalms put words to our thirst for vengeance and offers that in praying these psalms, we process our rage and give our violent impulses to God. *Psalm 58: 6, 8 (Good News Translation)* takes us there with, "*O God, break the teeth in their mouths; let them be like the snail that dissolves into slime.*" Cooledge declares that she supports this kind of prayer, and she is for praying the entire range of the Psalms — even the ones that sometimes make us uncomfortable or aren't welcome in church. She concludes, "If there is an occasion for an

Call for The Imprecatory Prayer Warrior

imprecatory psalm, the invasion by Russia and all of its relentless carnage gives occasions to tie these actions to the Psalms and let them allow God to exact justice in the way that God so chooses."[28] I concur, for this is the call of the imprecatory prayer warrior--to lay the tracks of life over the Word of Life; and expect a God conclusion that will be life-changing. These drastic times call for drastic prayer measures.

To close out this current twenty-first century perspective, I share Trevin Wax's commentary on C.S. Lewis, whom he strongly asserts that Lewis got it wrong as it concerns the imprecatory psalms. He writes, "Lewis thought these Psalms "devilish," naive, "diabolical," given to "pettiness" and "vulgarity." He believed their "vindictive hatred" to be contemptible—full of "festering,

---

[28] Liz Cooledge Jenkins, Sojourners Magazine 2024, Praying the Imprecatory Psalms Is an Act of Nonviolence

gloating, undisguised" passions that can in no way be "condoned or approved."[29] Further, he accuses Lewis of waffling on his perspective because Lewis still secured a teaching platform for these ancient songs while ruling them out of bounds for Christians.

With even more research on the subject, Christians may still question the relevancy of these Scriptures today. Should they be embedded in our prayer language as part of our personal and corporate worship experiences? Did New Testament theology somehow supersede them? If so, where? Wax provides home run clarity as he reminds us, "Jesus quotes from imprecatory *Psalm 69:9* in *John 2:17*. In *John 15:25*, Jesus also quotes *Psalms 35:19* and *64:9*, both of which are imprecatory psalms. This is not an exhaustive list; therefore, it is strange to claim that

---

[29] Trevin Wax, "The Gospel Coalition," 2024, "What C. S. Lewis Got Wrong About the Cursing Psalms, What C. S. Lewis Got Wrong About the Cursing Psalms (thegospelcoalition.org)

Call for The Imprecatory Prayer Warrior

because of the coming of Christ, we should no longer sing or pray the very songs Christ had no trouble singing or praying? Moreover, the Bible ends with a book that includes petitions for God to destroy the wicked (Rev 20:6,14). My belief rests on Wax's deduction and thoroughly supports praying prayers of imprecation. I am no stranger to putting on the clothes of the imprecatory prayer warrior and showing up in my prayer closet, passionately praying what God has spoken which provides answers and grants relief to ensure that justice is meted out in the many challenging situations whereas a pastor, I am called to entreat. Furthermore, I reach for them with intentionality for myself; for God to intervene where egregious, wanton, and reckless behaviors have prevailed. When one has seen great suffering and has experienced the same, one understands that inhumanity may need to be dealt with more swiftly and effectively by the Creator of humanity; and

Call for The Imprecatory Prayer Warrior

not by humanity itself. And how do we accomplish that? We go to God in His own Word, a Word that shall not return; with a specialized Word defined as the imprecatory prayer—spiritual weaponry akin to a Patriot missile overtaking a Scud missile.

Herein, I have provided a litany of resources to help you become comfortable in wielding the sword of the Word in imprecations. Don't deny yourself the privilege of a Davidian experience, where in *Psalm 58:6-8, David asks God to break the fangs of his enemies, make their weapons useless; and make them disappear like water into thirsty ground.* And God did! I have no problem approaching God with David's exact words, in order to experience the same justice, and neither should you!

Call for The Imprecatory Prayer Warrior

TODAY'S NEED FOR IMPRECATION PSALMS

Although the Bible is still the nation's bestselling book, many yet serve only to decorate the room rather than the soul. Desensitization of goodness now rules; with world secularism watering down the Word of God. But God has given the Word, that societies might be complete and healthy. Instead, we are failing in divine health with the worst crimes committed being humanity against humanity, nation against nation, family against family, race against race, denomination against denomination, neighborhood against neighborhood. Children are not safe at home anymore. They are subject to molestation and beyond, teen pregnancy, drugs, alcohol, and deception of every nature. We are not safe anywhere anymore. The medical community can treat our symptoms, but God is the only Healer.

Call for The Imprecatory Prayer Warrior

How, then, do societies access this God? Most people would say, "through his Word." That begs the question, "Do you mean all of His Word or some of His Word?" If it is the latter, one could perhaps legitimately support an opposing view of imprecation. However, since it is not, one would do well to seek ways to reconcile one's thinking to the infinite glory of God; and cease treating God as if He is stupid by declaring that He has given the world something that it cannot use.

So, how does one fix oneself? There was a woman who sought the solace of God through the Psalms after she experienced betrayal and adultery between her husband and her pastor's wife. The attitude of the perpetrators was immoral, wanton, and reckless. The humiliation and torment of the deception was so great that the woman entered therapy to deal with feelings that ran the gambit of homicide and suicide. Her psychiatrist prescribed medication to arrest her ongoing anxiety. Still, she could not find rest, thinking, "How could they; and God, how could you allow this to happen to me?" One night, she picked up the Bible and began to peruse the scriptures, particularly the Psalms. She somehow seemed to have been guided directly to *Psalm* 139. The language of slaying the wicked and moving the bloodthirsty in *Verse* 19 appeared to calm the emotional voice that was screaming within her for relief, where in the silence of her mind, she hoped that they both would die. However, she found it very difficult to pray the seemingly harsh favor of God to remove the gall and wormwood that had welled up within her, for she had not learned how to throw the total weight of the Word that she did not understand, back on God. The church had not taught her to do so. The Spirit led her to the medicine of imprecation, but she abandoned it. Was this a hindrance to her healing? Who

Call for The Imprecatory Prayer Warrior

knows? The Holy Spirit led her there. Furthermore, God might have given her what she needed. Nevertheless, this attitude is pervasive among Christians because of the need for sound doctrine in this area. Pauls reminds us that "imprecations call us to recognize the role of anger in dealing with suffering."[30] While I believe that therapy can assist, guide, suggest, and help you manage trauma, I hold fast to the belief that healing comes from God, who is our Healer. How do we access that healing? That healing is accessed through the Word of God, and for this matter, the imprecatory psalms. The woman in the story needed that *Psalm139:19* prescription. One needs the depth and breadth of God's Word to get through some of life's roughest spots. Yes, imprecation psalms have caused some to feel uncomfortable. However, *it takes the foolishness of God to*

---

[30] Pauls.

Call for The Imprecatory Prayer Warrior

confound those who are wise in their thinking (1 Cor. 1:27 KJV). Thus, it makes sense that God uses discomfort to produce His comfort.

So, what approach does one take? I have been an active participant in the faith community since I was eight years old; that's more than sixty years. My participation has included fellowship with most Christian denominations. I have attended and participated in thousands of religious teachings and preaching events. Until I entered graduate school, I had not heard anyone speak on the subject or suggest any readings and/or research on imprecatory scriptures. Once I was introduced to this subject through a seminary assignment, a whole new prayer world opened to me. I chose the topic for my first graduate research paper. I performed extensive researched on this genre of poetry located primarily in the Psalms, and in other books of the Bible as well.

Call for The Imprecatory Prayer Warrior

I was able to glean the schools of thought on the subject. As a poet, I felt a kindred connection with these Psalms. I was able to relate to the imagery and metaphors that some literally view as hate speech. Now that I am comfortable with imprecatory theology; and have experienced the benefit of it in my own life; I gift my learning and knowledge to every reader of this chapter, that you may be similarly blessed.

In this chapter, I offer three actions necessary to move teaching forward. The first is preachers and teachers must begin teaching these psalms as part of their spiritual programs. However, before they begin, they must pray for divine guidance to understand these scriptures in order to develop curriculums. Thus, preachers and teachers may need to educate or reeducate themselves in this particular area. Secondly, I encourage the readers of this chapter to engage study of the Word as your own personal spiritual discipline. Don't wait until you can find the right study group. Begin on your own. We live in times where a vast number of credible resources are immediately available to us. We must engage technology as a tool of study that we may do our best to *present ourselves to God, as one approved; a worker who does not need to be ashamed and who correctly handles the word of truth.* (2 Tim 2:15 NIV). We must continue to study the Word; because "*Blessed are those who hunger and thirst for justice; for they will be satisfied.*" (Mat 5:6 NLT). The third and final recommendation is that faith institutions must create a pastoral care environment that will offer opportunities for the body to assess and access the mysteries, miracles, and healing that come only through God's Word, allowing for teachings on the imprecation Psalms. To act on the third recommendation, the theological and faith communities must view the vengeance

Call for The Imprecatory Prayer Warrior

expressed in Old Testament imprecations to the precepts and teachings of the New Testament. I believe that in order to experience a supernatural result of healing, the church and theological community must engage and apply spiritual concepts, holding the mindset that a limitless God has not given us limited perspectives. Communities must accept that imprecations found in the Psalms are today's Balm in Gilead--spiritual salve for the wounded, tired souls who have depleted worldly antidotes, but hold out for the hope that God provides through all of His Word.

The motivation for imprecatory psalms is for God's Name, His glory, and His kingdom, not personal vindication. The imprecatory psalm does not seek to punish the wicked but commends them to God's judgment. The first hope of the imprecatory psalm is that God will so move the hearts of His enemies that they turn from their evil ways. Paul wrote, "All

Call for The Imprecatory Prayer Warrior

Scripture is given by inspiration of God and is profitable for doctrine, for proof, for correction, for instruction in righteousness." (II Tim 3:16). He did not say all scripture, except the imprecatory psalms, are good for doctrine. The imprecatory psalms are one more weapon in God's arsenal for combating evil. The world would do well to devote more time, study, and prayer to imprecatory psalms. Writers can often fall into the trap of beating a subject to death, where there is broad scholarly acceptance. Nonetheless, some are called to deal with uncomfortable truths. I am one of them. I pray that this information will catalyze a new prayer approach that will result in the readers' long-awaited renewal and healing. Dr. Charles Pitts, Old Testament Seminary Professor, always related regurgitating the Word to beading a necklace. He would urge us to create a masterpiece of jewels to hang about our necks. I pass that encouragement on to everyone reading this chapter. I leave you with a prayer necklace. This is how you will bead the necklace of the imprecatory prayer warrior.

First, consider what you are asking in prayer. In other words, will this be a prayer that decomposes national enemies, societal enemies, or personal enemies? Remember, that God declares in Ex 20:22 (NIV), "*I will be an enemy to your enemies and will oppose those who oppose you.*" Romans: 8:7-21 (GNT), reminds us that people become enemies of God when they are controlled by human nature; and do not obey God's law. Who are your enemies? They are the world, the flesh, and the devil—*the lust of the eye, the lust of the flesh, and the pride of life* (1John 2:15-17 NIV). Remember, the enemy is not flesh and blood. It is not necessarily the person or thing who has injured you; it is the spirit of evil that dwells therein. Consequently, it is necessary to execute spiritual warfare to destroy a negative spiritual presence. So, whether you bead a national, societal, or personal necklace; or a layered necklace where you are praying for all of these; this is how you begin. I will help you bead a necklace for the prayer below directed toward personal enemies. The jewels on this prayer necklace are *Isa 59, Mat 16:19, Ps 35, Ps 69, Heb 13:8, Mat 6:12, Is 55:11, 1Cor 15:18, and Lam 3:19*. Remember, when you are beading your necklace, use the Scriptures that speak to you and your situation. That could be an entire chapter, or certain scriptures that are unique to your circumstances. It's your necklace. Refer back to the section of this chapter that cites the Psalms that speak to personal enemies. Also allow the Holy Spirit to guide you to other text. Bead what you need; but include the imprecatory psalms that we have identified in this chapter as well. In so doing, for your part, you will have tied the Word you need about your neck and written it upon the table of your heart; placing

Call for The Imprecatory Prayer Warrior

yourself in position to experience a move of God!!!!!!! In so doing, you will be dressed in the clothing of the imprecatory prayer warrior; while the uncompromising Word of God, who is God, fights your battles; whereby you will cry, "I am victorious."

A PRAYER FOR YOU

Great God Almighty, Creator of the world and everything in it, I am blessed to be able to cry out to an awesome God whose ear is not too dull to hear me and whose arm is not too short to pull me up (Is 59:1 NIV). I am emotional in this hour. My heart is broken. If I could express my feelings, they would come forth as howls, accompanied by bottomless tears. The weight of my emotional baggage binds me. But I bind that weight here on earth; so that you will bind it in heaven; and I loose calmness, clarity, and collectedness over myself that it might be loosed back to me from heaven (Mat 16:19 NIV). Thank you for helping me to understand that there are divine prescriptions bottled in the Word of God that represent the "only" healing that will break the hold of pain, depression, disappointment, and downward spiraling that is upon me in this hour because my enemies

Call for The Imprecatory Prayer Warrior

seek to destroy me, my work, my character, my value, my purpose, my mission, my soul. Thus, I decree Psalm 35 in its entirety over myself and the issues that beset me, understanding that you LORD, will contend with those who fight against me, putting them to shame and disgrace; and turning them back in dismay. My tongue will proclaim your righteousness and your praises all day long. (Jer 33, Ps 91). Please relieve me from this grief just as you relieved David's grief expressed in Psalm 69. I decree the entirety of this psalm over myself, as I echo David's cry to a God (The Word), who is the same yesterday today and forevermore (Heb 13:8 NIV). Lord, forgive my debts as I forgive my debtors (Mat 6:12 NKJB). God, you said if we decree a thing it would be established (Job 22:28). I have decreed the Word, so let your Word be established in my life, for your Word does not return void, but it will accomplish that which you desire; and achieve the purpose for which you sent it (Is 55:11 NIV). I stand steadfast (1Cor 15:58 NIV); as You, The Word, fight my battles; until this wormwood and gall are lifted from me (Lamentations 3:19 NIV). Thank you in advance for allowing the Word to penetrate my inward parts, bringing me resolution and restoration (Psalm 139). I praise you! I thank you! I give you glory! In the precious name of your Son, Jesus! Amen!"

Call for The Imprecatory Prayer Warrior

A CALL TO ACTION

Now, that you can move from an informed space, you are ready for action. If you desire to become an imprecatory prayer warrior, below are three steps toward activating your call.

1. Commit yourself to praying about all that you have learned in this chapter; and ask God to show you that this is all part of the healing thread that comes from God's Word.

2. Decide on the area or areas that you want to address through imprecatory prayer--whether it is personal, societal, or national. You may be facing circumstances in one or all of these areas, where the enemy is wreaking havoc in your life. Choose one or choose all of them.

3. Select imprecatory Scriptures from the information provided in this chapter that speaks to personal, societal, and national enemies. Choose one category or layer your necklace:

but bead God's Word among your jewels. The Word addresses your enemies, allows you to lament, and it throws the sword of God's vengeance, correction, or resolutions to God, who fights for you; and then hands you the victory.

I urge you to put on the prayer beads of the imprecatory prayer warrior and pray.

BIBLIOGRAPHY

Anderson, Gary A. "King David and the Psalms of Imprecation." Pro Ecclesia 15. no. 3, October 2006: 267-280.

Ashmon, Scott A. "The Wrath of God: A Biblical Overview." Concordia Journal 31, no. 4, October 2005: 348-358.

Bratcher, Dennis. "List of "Types of Psalms Classifying the Psalms by Genre." 2018. https://www.crivoice.org/psalmtypehtml. (accessed September 23, 2024).

Brueggemann, Walter. Message of the Psalms. Mineapolis: Ausburg, 1984.

Crenshaw, James L. "The Reification of Divine Evil." Perspectives in Religious Studies 28, no.4, (Winter 2001z): 327-332.

Day, John N. "The Imprecatory Psalms and Christian Ethics." Bibliotheca Sacra 159, no. 634, April - June 2002: 166-186.

Declaisse'-Walford, Nancy L. An Introduction to the Psalms: A Psalm from Ancient Israel. St. Louis: Chalice Press, 2004.

Eidsmoe, John. Imprecation? Biblical? Christian? Christanity, Law, Miscellaneous, Morality, Speech, Uncategorized, Firm Foundation. n.d. http://morallaw.org/blog (accessed May 9, 2009).

Fretheim, Terence E. "I Was a Little Angry: Divine Violence in the Prophets." Interpretation 50. no.4, (October 2004): 62.

Gaiser, Frederick J. "Deliver Us from Evil." Word and World 22, no. 1, (Winter 2002): 3-5.

Goldengay, John. Psalms 3 Volumes: Baker Commentary on the Old Testament Widsom Psalms. Grand Rapids: Baker Academic, 2006, 2007. 2008.

Harrison, Ronald K. Introduction to the Old Testament. Grand Rapids: Erdmans Publishng Company, 1969.

Jacobs, Steven L. "Mabul, Hurricanes, Tsunamis, Earthquakes, Shoah, and Genocide: Acts of a Vengeful God?" Council of Societies for the Study of Religion Bulletin 35, no.3, (January - May 1980) 35-45.

Jenkins, Liz Coolege. "Praying the Imprecatory Psams Is an Act of Nonviolence." Sojouorners Magazine, 2024.

Kelley, Page H. "Prayers of the Troubled Saints." Review and Expositor 81, no. 3, (September 2006): 375.

Laney, Carl J. "A Fresh Look at the Imprecatory Psalms." Bibliotheca Sacra 138, no. 549, (January - May 1980): 35-45.
Leupold, H. C. The Psalms. Baker Book House, 1969.

Matthew 5:38-44 (KJV)." 2011.

McCann, J. Clinton. "The Psalmistry: Psalms 44." Brill, 2002.

Mitchell, David C. "God Will Redeem my Soul from Sheol: The Psalms of the Sons of Korah." Journal for the Study of the Old Testament 30, no.3, (March 2006): 365 and 528.

Modahl, Bruce K. "From Wrath to Grace." Christian Century 116, no.30, (November 3, 1999): 1051.

Mosher, Barry. "Blood and Stone: Violence in the Bible and the Eye of the Illustrator." Cross Currents 51, no. 2, (Summer 2001): 219-228.

Pauls, Gerald. The Imprecations of the Psalmist: A Study of Psalm 54. Fall 1993. http://directionjournal.org/article/806 (accessed May 8, 2009).

Pitts, Charles. Ph.D. "Lectures from Old Testament 721 Class." Houston, March 5, 2009.

"Psalm 109:9 (NIV)." 2011.

"Psalm 58:6 (NIV)." 2011.

Reed, Lessing. "Broken Teeth, Bloody Baths, and Baby Bashing, Is There Any Place in the Church for Imprecatory

Psalms?" Concordia Journal 32, no.4, (October 2006): 368-370.

Rosencrans, Emily Duncan. "The Source of Our Strength." Journal for Preachers 26 no.4, (Pentecost 2003): 5-19.

Stienhauser, Jaroslav Pelikan and A.T.W., ed. The Sermon on the Mount and the Magnificat. Vol. 21. n.d.

Storm, Sam. Enjoying God Ministries, Biblical Theological Resources from the Ministry of Dr. Sam, Those Troubling Psalms of Imprecation. n.d. http://enjoyin.

Thomas, Robert L. "The Imprecatory Prayers of the Apocalypse." Bibliotheca Sacra 126, no. 502, n.d.

Wagner, Christine B. Scholastic Answers, In Defense of Imprecatory Psalms. September 2024. http://christinewagner.com (accessed September 2024).

Wax, Trevin. What C. S. Lewis Got Wrong About the Cursing Psalms. 2024. thegospelcoalition.org (accessed September 2024).

Call for The Imprecatory Prayer Warrior

ABOUT THE CONTRIBUTOR

Dr. Benda Arnold-Scott is a Houston native, began her writing journey in 1988, with her early works featured in several anthologies including The Sounds of Poetry and Bittersweet Rhapsody by Howard Ely. A graduate of Texas Southern University with a B.B.A. in Marketing, she is a life member of Delta Mu Delta and Beta Gamma Sigma honor fraternities. With nearly 30 years of experience in urban development, Brenda also serves as an Ordained Elder in the AME Church and has been in pastoral ministry for over 20 years. She holds a Master of Divinity from Houston Graduate School of Theology and a Doctor of Ministry in Urban Communities and Social Justice from Southern Methodist University. A retired community development professional, she is multi-talented, and still making a difference as a pastor, author, poet, and advocate. She

Call for The Imprecatory Prayer Warrior

continues to contribute to numerous fields, including philanthropy and entrepreneurship, while aiming to share more of her literary works from the past 25 years.

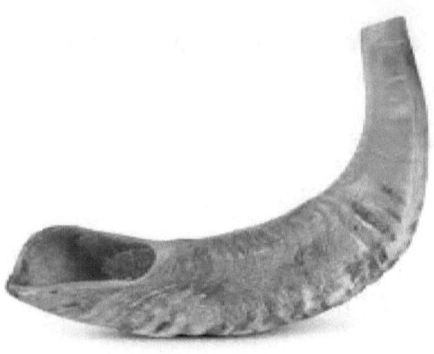

2

CALL FOR THE LEADERSHIP INTERCESSOR

Likeythia Blackmon, B.S., M. Ed

Praying for your leaders is a wonderful way to support them in ministry. Leaders often carry heavy spiritual, emotional, and practical burdens as they lead the congregation. Prayer can offer strength, wisdom and encouragement. There are many areas we can generally pray for our leaders: their health, guidance, discernment, personal relationships, and the ability to lead with love and grace.

It is my belief that the true call to pray effectual, fervent prayers for our leaders comes first from being in the church God has called us, as the worshippers/servants to be. Joining a church is not based on how live the worship team is, or how lit (if that is still the term) the band is. It is not even the fact that the church offers the ministries we love or that capture our interest. Serving in a ministry or church is solely about being where God has assigned, predetermined for us to be. We should know that when we disobey God by not being where He has called us to be and by not doing what He has called us to do, we are unfaithful to God, and we are not in unity or alignment with His plans for our lives. However, when we return and get "in line with God's will," God invites us to repentance and

Call for The Leadership Intercessor

as He told Israel in Jeremiah 3:14-15, "*Return, you faithless sons, declares the Lord; For I am a master to you. And I will take you, one from a city and two from a family, And bring you to Zion. Then I will give you shepherds after my own heart, who will feed you knowledge and understanding.*" When we reach this point, then and only then can we move forward with the call God had placed on our lives.

Now, as we have established that our place of worship is not a decision that happens haphazardly or based on things that appeal to our human nature but is an assignment from God, let's move forward in our call to praying for leadership. When we are called to pray for our leadership, we must make sure, through prayer, fasting, and discernment, we have our hearts and minds in tune to God.

Praying for our leaders goes beyond praying for houses, cars, money, and all the other

Call for The Leadership Intercessor

tangibles we can think of. While there is nothing wrong with praying for our leaders to have these things, our pastors face a plethora of challenges daily, that are spiritual, in the heavenly realm, so interceding on our leader's behalf is a must. According to Richard J. Foster in Celebration of Discipline, "Your pastor and the services of worship need to be bathed in prayer. Paul prayed for his people; he asked his people to pray for him. Charles Spurgeon attributed his success to the prayers of his church. Frank Laubach told his audiences, I am very sensitive, and I know whether you are praying for me."[31] When we pray for our leaders, we must spend time with God, seeking Him for what to pray for.

For the sake of this anthology, we will look at one of the scriptures in the bible that tells us about the role of a pastor. From this scripture,

---

[31] Richard Foster. *Celebration of Discipline The Path to Spiritual Growth*. Harper One. (New York, NY: HarperCollins Publishers, 1998), 43.

Call for The Leadership Intercessor

I'd like to unpack a set of prayer target we could bring to God in prayer on behalf of our leaders. Before we begin unpacking, I would like to share just a little bit as to why I believe I have been called to pray for leadership. According to Merriam-Webster Dictionary, a call is a divine vocation or strong inner prompting to a particular course of action. As long as I have been serving in church, I have had a call to pray for leadership; it did not matter where I served. Presently, that call is as strong as it was when I first experienced it. I will share that it was through prayer and discernment that I realized not everyone experiences this calling. Originally, it was not clear to me that it was a calling. I had to depend a lot on *John 10: 27, "My sheep listen to My voice, and I know them, and they follow Me."* This verse is a staple because there are times when God is speaking and we are not sure what to do, but we trust Him because we know His voice. The knowing of God's voice comes

Call for The Leadership Intercessor

from spending time with Him in prayer. I wanted to share a snippet about my calling because I believe that someone reading this may be struggling with the call. You are feeling that tug, that urge to pray but you are unsure of what to do. Just pray. Stop and pray. I know this is new for you or just different. Trust God, He is leading you. He is calling you to pray.

Preparation for this anthology has been a labor of love. Daily I have found myself in thought and prayer regarding this work. My thoughts were always encompassed in my desire for this work to be relevant and relatable. My desire was for the reader to understand it and for it not to become too cumbersome to understand. In my opinion, prayer is simple, it does not have to be complex language—it is a conversation between you and God and that is what I wanted this chapter to reflect.

Call for The Leadership Intercessor

Day after day, I would lose time, praying about what this chapter would reflect. Honestly, I believe I spent more time in prayer than writing the chapter. Why you might ask. The answer is simple. Because it is so important to me that the message is clear, concise, and received. Praying for our leaders is imperative. As we work through the very important call to pray for leadership, we must know that all leaders are not receptive to the call of prayer. Personally, I have experienced both, leaders who welcomed the call on my life to pray for them and leaders who were not as excited about that call.

Not all leaders are the same, and neither are their priorities. As an intercessor for your leaders, you will quickly learn that, but it still your job to pray until God releases you from that assignment and gives permission to move on to the next one. Unfortunately, moving on from one assignment to the next is not your

Call for The Leadership Intercessor

decision, it is God's. He is the one with the plan. To be released from an assignment is not the same as being released from a church. There are times when God will have you to specifically pray for something for your leaders or pray for a specific area in their lives. When God says move on to the next area or prayer target, we must be so in tune with the Holy Spirit that we know when to move on.

As we prepare to move into our prayer targets to intercede on behalf of our leaders, I have provided some sample prayer targets below. These are sample targets to help frame your thoughts when thinking about praying for your leadership. I would like to remind us that prayer is simply communication with God. It is a time we spend sharing with and listening to God. We, most of the time, divulge this list of wants, needs, hurts, pains, etc. But in this anthology, I would like to take the opportunity to share with you the blueprint scripture, on

Call for The Leadership Intercessor

how to pray for our leaders. I call it a blueprint because it tells us about the office of a pastor and provides us with a great example of how to combat the enemy, hence giving us a sample of prayer targets. According to I Timothy 3: 1-7, *It is a trustworthy statement: if any man aspires to the office of [a]overseer, it is a fine work he desires to do. ² An overseer, then, must be above reproach, the husband of one wife, temperate, self-controlled, respectable, hospitable, skillful in teaching, ³ not overindulging in wine, not a bully, but gentle, not contentious, free from the love of money. ⁴ He must be one who manages his own household well, keeping his children under control with all dignity ⁵ (but if a man does not know how to manage his own household, how will he take care of the church of God?), ⁶ and not a new convert, so that he will not become conceited and fall into condemnation incurred by the devil. ⁷ And he must have a good reputation with those*

Call for The Leadership Intercessor

outside the church, so that he will not fall into disgrace and the snare of the devil. I Timothy 3:1-7 is a powerful scripture to use when praying for leadership because it outlines the essential qualities and spiritual maturity required of leaders/pastors, and as previously mentioned, it gives us a great example of how to war in prayer for our leaders.

PRAYER TARGETS

Target: Above Reproach (disapproval or disappointment), husband of one wife, temperate, self-control, respectable, hospitable, skillful in teaching.

Scriptures: Colossians 1:22; Galatians 5:16-25; I Timothy 6; II Timothy 2:15, Proverbs 15: 1-2; John 21: 15-19

Explanation: Praying for your leader to be "above reproach" is praying for your leader's character, leadership, and actions in general to be aligned with biblical standards. Being above reproach means to be blameless or free

Call for The Leadership Intercessor

from accusations that could "discredit" their leadership or witness.

Sample Prayer: *Dear Lord, I thank you for my leader(s). I thank you for my leader(s) humble spirit. Lord, I thank you because my leader(s) loves their spouse and is faithful to their marriage vows. I know that situations arise regarding the church, but I thank that my leader(s) lives out the fruit of the spirit, in the name of Jesus. Father, I give you honor for the time You have given my leader(s) to study Your word. Not only in preparation for preaching and teaching, but for life that my leader(s) will be able to make it on this journey when things arise. Lord, I thank You that You have kept my leader(s) blameless before men. In the name of Jesus, Amen.*

Thought(s):

_____

_____

_____

Target: Not overindulging in wine, not a bully, gentle, not contentious (likely to cause disagreement or argument), free from the love of money.

Call for The Leadership Intercessor

Scriptures: Proverbs 20:1; Galatians 5:16-25; Matthew 22:37-38, Proverbs 15:1-2

Explanation: This prayer target is important because leaders must be spiritually clear-headed to make wise decisions, guide the congregation, and live a life of holiness and humility. Gentleness is also very important for leaders. We want to cover them in prayer in this area as they navigate many people, situations, and circumstances.

Sample Prayer: *Oh, Lord, Our God! I thank for my leader(s) sobriety. Father, I thank you that my leader(s) chooses to keep sober in mind and spirit that he/she may be wise in their decisions. Dear Lord, I thank you that my leader(s) know that a soft answer turns away wrath, and even when my leader(s) wants to respond, they defer to You. And, dear Lord, I thank you that my leader(s) loves You and your people more that money. I am so thankful that my leader(s) loves you with all his/her heart. In mighty name of Jesus, Amen.*

Thought(s):

_____

_____

_____

Call for The Leadership Intercessor

Target: Manages his own household well.

Scriptures: James 1:5; Proverbs 22:6; Proverbs 15:1-2

Explanation: When praying for your leader to manage his/her household well, you are praying for your leader to seek God for the ability to lead their family with respect, authority, and order. This also can honestly cover multiple practical areas: organization, decision-making, ability to set boundaries. You are also covering your leader(s) in prayer in these areas.

Sample Prayer: *Father in heaven, I thank you for a leader who seeks You for wisdom in all things. Father, I thank you because my leader(s) needs Your wisdom leading Your people, being a faithful spouse to one, raising their children, on their job, and everywhere they go. Thank you for being faithful to my leader(s) and trusting him/her with the wisdom, knowledge and understanding needed to do what you have called them to. In Jesus's name, Amen.*

Thought(s):

_____

_____

_____

Call for The Leadership Intercessor

Target: Not a new convert, not fall into condemnation.

Scriptures: Ephesians 6:10-18; I Timothy 6; II Timothy 2:15

Explanation: This prayer target is crucial because one of the key responsibilities of leaders is to teach sound doctrine; you want to cover this area in prayer because sound doctrine is important for the spiritual growth of the church—it is essential.

Sample Prayer: *Father in heaven, I ask that you cover my leader(s) from the crown of his/her head to the soles of their feet. Please allow no hurt, harm or danger to come near my leader(s) nor their dwelling place. Dear Lord, I thank you for giving my leader(s) wisdom and time to study your word and understand as well. Dear Lord, please help my leader(s) to rightly divide the word and keep his/her ear and heart in tune with You. Father, I thank you because my leader(s) does not take away or add to Your word but stays true to what You say. In the name of Jesus, Amen.*

Thought(s):

_____

Call for The Leadership Intercessor

_____

_____

Target: Have a good reputation outside the church; not fall into disgrace; not fall into the snare of the devil.

Scriptures: Matthew 5:16; Galatians 5:22-23; I Corinthians 15:33; Romans 12:17; Philippians 4:8; Proverbs 16:18

Explanation: Praying for our leaders to have a good reputation is important because it directly impacts their effectiveness in ministry. We do not want our leader's character or integrity to be called into question. We cover in this area because we want our leader's lives to reflect God wherever they go.

Sample Prayer: *All mighty God, I thank You for Your divine protection. I thank you for keeping my leader(s); protecting him/her from the enemy and from anything within that could arise and cause my leader(s) to walk contrary to You. Father, I thank You that his/her mind is covered, and he/she thinks on pure and honorable things. Father, I thank you that my leader(s) does not seek vengeance, but knows that vengeance belongs to you, and Father, I thank you that my leader(s) is humble and*

Call for The Leadership Intercessor

allows Your light to shine. In the mighty name of Jesus I pray, Amen.

Thought(s):

_____

_____

_____

As we have concluded our prayer targets, please remember to pray for your leader(s); they need it. As previously stated, while they appreciate the prayers for the tangibles, it's the intangibles that really make the difference for the Bible says in *Ephesians* 6:12, "*For our struggle is not against flesh and blood, but against the rulers, against the powers, against the world forces of this darkness, against the spiritual forces of wickedness in the heavenly places.*"

The call to intercede on behalf of our leaders is not always pleasant or easy. Sometimes it is difficult. In Adele Calhoun's Spiritual

Call for The Leadership Intercessor

Discipline's Handbook, she states, "Intercession is not always an easy thing to do. It can engage us deeply in the spiritual battle. Intercessors know that the point of intercessory prayer is to remain faithful and trusting. Being involved in intercessory prayer does not necessarily mean you'll feel great strength, power, or joy. The point is to pray, persist, and commit the battle to the Lord."[32]

Answer the call!

A CALL TO ACTION

As you reflect on this chapter, Call for the Leadership Intercessor, I encourage you to make a deliberate and consistent effort to cover your leaders in prayer. Pastors carry immense, responsibility in guiding, teaching, and caring for the flock God has given them; their work is spiritually, and oftentimes

---

[32] Adele Calhoun. *Spiritual Disciplines Handbook Practices That Transform Us.* (Downers Grove, IL: InterVarsity Press, 2005), 232.

Call for The Leadership Intercessor

emotionally demanding. Their work is also, a lot of the times, unseen.

By praying for your leadership, you support their strength, wisdom, and resilience in fulfilling their calling. Please, take a moment, daily, to pray for your leaders. These prayers can not only cover the targets delineated above, but also pray for their physical health, emotional well-being and spiritual strength. Our prayers are a powerful source of encouragement, so let us commit to covering those who lead us, in prayer. **Answer the call!**

A PRAYER FOR YOU

Dear Heavenly Father, Thank You for the person reading these words, who has taken the time to read this chapter and seek Your guidance in prayers for their leadership. I pray that You would bless them with a heart full of compassion, wisdom, and understanding as they cover their pastors/leaders in prayer. May they be a

Call for The Leadership Intercessor

source of encouragement and support, knowing that their prayers are extremely important, a vital part of their leader's spiritual strength. May their prayers bring comfort and power to their leaders and may both the reader and their leadership grow stronger in faith and to the mission You have called them to. In Jesus's name, Amen.

BIBLIOGRAPHY

Calhoun, Adele Ahlberg. *Spiritual Disciplines Hanbook*. Downers Grove: IVP Books, 2005.

Foster, Richard J. *Celebration of Discipline*. New York: Harper One, 1998.

ABOUT THE CONTRIBUTOR

Minister Likeythia Blackmon is a dedicated member of New Direction Community Church, serving under the leadership of Pastor Cedric and First Lady Shante Francis. She actively contributes to the Prayer, Clean

Call for The Leadership Intercessor

Hearts, and Administration Ministries, and teaches Life Group, while always stepping in wherever she's needed. Likeythia is a proud mother of three adult children—Randy, Randryck, and LaRaneisha—and a loving mother-in-love to Candance. Her greatest joys, aside from her love for God, are her grandsons, Landon and Khaizer. With over 30 years of experience in education, Likeythia currently works as a Special Education Coordinator for Deaf and Hard of Hearing students within the Houston Independent School District. She holds a Bachelor's degree from Texas Southern University, a Master's degree and Graduate Certificate from Texas Tech University, and is pursuing advanced studies in Christian Spirituality and a Master of Divinity at the Houston Graduate School of Theology. Likeythia firmly believes that every aspect of her life, from ministry to profession, is divinely connected. This conviction has

Call for The Leadership Intercessor

shaped one of her guiding principles: "You should always be who you say you are."

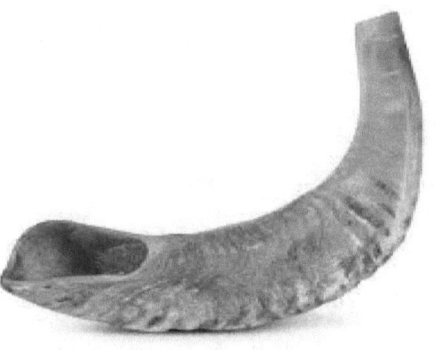

3

CALL FOR THE FASTING PRAYER

Dr. Rhonda Yvonne Green Harmon

As I begin to write this chapter on prayer and fasting, my focus is to help the people of God gain or increase a desire to learn more about the call for fasting and prayer. I am aware that I am still learning how to fast and pray. Each fast, along with prayer, is different for me and others. Whether it is a weekly fast with prayer or a continued fast with prayer, one must seek the face of God in reading and meditating on the Word of God initially and throughout the fast with much prayer. Many books written about prayer do not include fasting. I have read and consulted them throughout my lifetime. There are many books, retreats, and courses to teach prayer. There are vital Scriptures quoted from the Bible to remind us to pray. However, we are moving in this chapter as a beginner in some respect to another level or dimension of prayer that includes fasting. As disciples of Jesus Christ, we realize there is no quick fix or microwave results. We come as learners. We come as children of God seeking a more excellent way to communicate and pass the tests of life in the Name of Jesus.

As I teach and write about prayer and fasting, I know that people are leery of it and weary of praying and waiting on the results of their petitions to El Shaddai. I hold fast to some of

Call for The Fasting Prayer

my memories during these times of waiting for answers from God. I console myself with some quotes such as, "It's not in my time," "Pray without Ceasing," "Man (woman) ought always to pray," and one of the mainstays we quote - "He may not come when we want Him, but He is always on time." So, you see, I have been on this prayer journey with fasting for a very long time. I have also spent many years praying without fasting. So, are you ready to move deeper into your prayer life with fasting? I hear a yes.

Some may ask, why learn or increase knowledge of praying and fasting now? Will God still answer our prayers without fasting at the Divinely appointed time? Questions will arise as you read if you have never fasted and prayed before for the next level of discipline. Should I fast? Can I fast? How long do I have to fast? Who says prayer and fasting are essential? The questions can go on and on. In

Call for The Fasting Prayer

this chapter, I will attempt to answer some or many of my and your concerns. It is okay to underline and make notes in the margin or use a notebook for journal writing (which I am committed to helping others begin to journal) as you read and discern the times of prayer and fasting, according to *Mark 9:29 KJV*. As we learn and relearn, I pray that the Holy Spirit will be our teacher. *Luke 11:1 (KJV)* "Lord, *teach us to pray*" and '*this kind goeth not out but by prayer and fasting*" *Matthew 17:21 (KJV)*. We find that *Mark 9:29 KJV* and *Matthew 17:21 KJV* emphasize the necessity of prayer and fasting to overcome specific spiritual challenges.

In this chapter we will review and learn from our big sisters and brothers in the Old Testament and New Testament Scriptures along with the community of my faith we call the church. Our big sisters and big brothers serve as teachers with testimonials of trust and belief throughout Scripture. In our

Call for The Fasting Prayer

studying prayer and fasting, I am praying for us all to continue to be encouraged by our Great God. As we learn and relearn to understand that prayer and fasting is not only talking to God, or denying ourselves, but this journey will include listening. This prayer and fasting journey will allow us to see our lives change for the greater good of all humanity. I pray and fast as we come into this journey together, we will know that Abba Father is with us all the way. I pray and fast as we begin to connect and reconnect with God through prayer and fasting expectations of the deaf being able to hear, the blind receiving their sight, and the lame walking, in the Name of Jesus. O Hallelujah! Deliverance and transformation evolve into doing something new (*Isaiah* 43:19) and renewing our minds to delve deeper into the next prayer and fasting lifestyle of transformation through fasting and praying.

Call for The Fasting Prayer

I want to express my warm, heartfelt thanks and gratitude to my Lord and Savior, and to Dr. Tammy Isaac for inviting me to write this chapter in the Prayer Anthology with the other co-authors. Thank you for reading and listening to God throughout this chapter. I wish to extend my gratitude to the women and men whose personal stories in this chapter include practicing the spiritual discipline of prayer and fasting. Except where noted, I have changed names or omitted identifying facts and shaped stories to preserve confidentiality. Also, I am thankful to God for my husband, Exhorter, 1st Gentleman A.J., for his love, patience, helpfulness, and caring to walk alongside me on this journey. Thank You. Last and First is my Jehovah Jireh, Lord and Savior Jesus Christ Yeshua, along with the Holy Spirit, my angels assigned to bring all that I am and could ever hope to be into manifestation. Amen and Amen.

Call for The Fasting Prayer

SIGNIFICANT SCRIPTURES ON PRAYER AND FASTING

According to Study.com, prayer is mentioned 279 times in the New Testament.[33] Bible trivia questions answered by Phil Logos says that "in the KJV, a comprehensive count of all variations of the word pray, petition, supplication, and beseech results in 693 mentions in 614 verses. The ESV, which reserves the use of "pray" for instances of communication with God, yields 338 mentions in 302 verses. However, the Bible trivia shows no definitive answer to how often the word appears with related words and phrases.[34] According to Bible study tools.com, fasting is mentioned over 70 times throughout Scripture.[35] Prayer and fasting together are

---

[33] Study.com
[34] Phil Logos, "How many times is prayer mentioned in the Bible?". https://bibletrivia.co.uk/trivia/how-many-times-is-prayer-mentioned-in-the-bible
[35] The BibleStudyTools Staff on 1.15.24. https://www.biblestudytools.com/topical-verses/bible-verses-about-fasting/

mentioned approximately ten times together, according to Got Questions.org, under the question, "What is the connection between prayer and fasting? The following Scripture references from the King James Version of the Holy Bible are a.) *Daniel* 9: 3, b.) *Nehemiah chapter* 1, c.) *2 Samuel* 12:16, 21-22, d.) *Esther* 4:16, e.) *Luke* 2:37, f.) *Mark* 6:7, 9;21-22,29, g.) *Ephesians* 6:18, h.) *Hebrews* 10:19, there are a few more not listed here. [36] Let us plunge into the calling of fasting prayer by beginning with prayer.

WHAT IS PRAYER?

Bible trivia questions answered by Phil Logos in the article, " How many times is prayer mentioned in the Bible," says prayer is a fundamental aspect of religious practice and spiritual life, serving as a means of

---

[36] Got Questions Your Questions. Biblical Answers., "What is the connection between prayer and fasting?" https://www.gotquestions.org/prayer-fasting.html.

communication between believers and the divine.[37] According to the *Westminster Dictionary of Theological Terms*, prayer (from Latin *precari*, "to entreat") is a Human approach to God, addressing God in praise and adoration, confession, thanksgiving, supplication, and intercession. Some people may experience the consciousness of God's presence, love, direction, and grace.[38] According to the Dictionary/Concordance of the NIV Life Application Study Bible, prayer simply means communicating with God, as in many Scriptures.[39] In other words, prayer is simply talking to God like my mother, father, or a good friend. Prayer is a time spent as we mature by giving God back the Words written

---

[37] Phil Logos., "How many times is prayer mentioned in the Bible." https://bibletrivia.co.uk/trivia/howmany-times-is-prayermentioned-in-the-bible

[38] Donald K. McKim, *Westminster Dictionary of Theological Terms*, Westminster John Knox Press, Louisville, Kentucky, 1996, 1st Ed.216.

[39] NIV Life Application Study Bible. Copyright by Zondervan, Grand Rapids, Michigan, and co-published by Tyndale House Publishers, Inc. Carol Stream, Illinois. 2011.2348.

in the Bible that would fit the needs at the time.

WHAT IS FASTING?

Fasting is the key theme in this chapter of the prayer anthology. We are all discussing prayer with a purpose. My assignment is to press my case through the Word of God about the importance of fasting and prayer. I call it moving to the next level. Fasting does not pressure God or make God answer our prayers any faster. Fasting improves our clarity when hearing from God. Fasting deepens our relationships with God in the Name of Jesus.

Let me begin with my revelation from God on how to teach the discipline of fasting. I am thankful that El Shaddai has allowed me to approach fasting uniquely to the various congregations I have pastored. So many

Call for The Fasting Prayer

people in the church do not know or understand prayer and fasting. The desire is not there because of confusion and the lack of knowledge. The Almighty God has worked through me to get the people to understand that fasting can be the absence of anything we love. Fasting is more than abstaining from food and drink for some time. We can refrain from many things that we immediately say yes to daily.

The focus of fasting can start with the things in our lives that are addictive or habitual (smoking, gambling, social media, television, music -secular and gospel). Fasting can also begin with giving up sodas (other drinks that are not healthy) as well as different foods that we love. We fast to transform (change from our focus to the focus of God). Even though it has been my experience that if we are under the care of a doctor and directions to fast from midnight till our appointment, we do it (without a complaint), nevertheless, we do it because the earthly doctor said so. Yet, if the church is fasting or the pastor calls for a fast of nothing but water for eight to ten hours, some find many reasons this is not doable. I never ask anyone not to take their medication. If you need to eat to take your medication, then do so. Taking medication does not stop one from participating in a fast with prayer. Simply change what you are eating. The example I have given when we need to eat to take medication is the following: Eat a balanced meal (smaller portions of meat and vegetables- take away the rice, potatoes, bread, and dessert with water instead of sweet tea or soft drinks). This allows us to take the medication needed and still participate in a fast with prayer. This gives you a beginning to the discipline of prayer and fasting by taking away some of the foods we love.

Call for The Fasting Prayer

When we start where we are in prayer and fasting, we then can grow to give up more. The emphasis here is fasting. When asked to pray, usually, it is not rejected as much as fasting. However, the heart's desire is needed to pray and increase the discipline of how we pray. Our prayer life will grow as we move through the discipline of prayer by giving God back the Words found in Scripture as they apply to the situations and circumstances that we and others are facing. I give these suggestions as techniques and strategies for a beginner in prayer and fasting. I will expound on it in my personal testimony section. If we are consistent with giving up things we love through prayer and fasting, we can begin to live in freedom from habits and addictions.

Through research of the writings of James W. Goll, I find that this contemporary also expounds on the 21st-century issues of life that could be considered a form of sacrifice,

Call for The Fasting Prayer

abstinence, or "fasting" before God. The following list from James Goll is not representative of fasting from food. However, it is a form of fasting from issues of today's society for some time in seeking the Almighty God with prayer and fasting. They are the following:

1. Abstinence from sexual relationships (I Corinthians 7:5 KJV)
2. Entertainment; Movies, videos, television, radio, video games, secular dancing, etc.
3. Athletic Events-Professional sports, athletic events, other forms of recreation, etc.
4. Reading material from magazines, books, newspapers, other news media, and even Christian fiction.
5. Computers-Internet activity, E-mail, games, etc.
6. Speech- Phone calls, amount of talking, limiting topics of conversation, a special vow of silence, etc.
7. Dress- avoiding certain types and styles of clothing, or wearing specific types and styles of clothing, etc.
8. Foods and Drinks- Partial fasting limits the intake of specific foods or drinks.

9. Sleep-Early morning prayer, all-night prayer vigils, prayer watches at various hours, etc.
10. Social Functions-Limiting outside engagements, conferences, seminars, and normal church activities for short specific periods; time of purposeful isolation.
11. Work schedule hours of the day off from secular work or even ministry engagements to seek the face of God, etc.[40]

James W. Goll states the verb "fasting" comes from the Hebrew term tsum, which refers to self-denial. The noun tsum means voluntary abstinence from food. Goll continues to give evidence of fasting from the Bible. They are the following from the King James Version of the Holy Bible:

- Hannah (*I Samuel* 1:7); distressed
- King Ahab (*I Kings* 21:4); failure
- David (*II Samuel* 3:35); grief

---

[40] James W. Goll, James W. Goll, " Consecrated, Contemplative Prayer-The Fasted Life",
https://itsallaboutyeshua.wordpress.com/2013/09/24/consecrated-contemplative-prayer-the-fasted-life-by-james-w-goll/

Call for The Fasting Prayer

- The Day of Atonement (*Leviticus* 16:11,15,21,29); required fast; Day of Atonement

Goll reminds us that when fasting became a national call, it was to seek divine favor, protection, or circumvent God's historical judgment.[41] However, according to the Westminster Dictionary of Theological Terms, the definition of fasting is " Abstinence from food for religious devotion and spiritual discipline."[42] Also, the dictionary says fast days mean "Days when people refrain from eating solid food because of religious convictions or particular spiritual concerns." Their purpose is often to enhance one's sense of God's presence. They may also be for penance or repentance, regularly or as perceived needs arise.[43] In the Dictionary/Concordance of the NIV Life Application Study Bible, fasting

---

[41] Goll.
[42] Donald K. McKim, "Westminster Dictionary of Theological Terms," Westminster John Knox Press, Louisville, Kentucky, 1996, 1st Ed.102.
[43] Ibid.,102.

Call for The Fasting Prayer

means "to abstain from food, especially as a religious discipline." Scriptures that refer to fasting in the NIV version of the Bible are Psalm 35:13, Matthew 6:16, Acts 13:2, and Acts 14:23.[44]

The writings of Elmer L. Towns inspire nine Biblical Fasts in his book *Fasting for Spiritual Breakthrough*, recorded by James W. Goll. I will only give the title of the fast and the Scriptures used for each. They are as follows:

1. The Disciples Fast-Isaiah 58:6, Matthew 17:21 (KJV)
2. The Ezra Fast-Isaiah 58:6, Ezra 8:23 (KJV)
3. The Samuel Fast-Isaiah 58:6, I Samuel 7:6 (KJV)
4. The Elijah Fast-Isaiah 58:6, I Kings 19:4,8 (KJV)
5. The Widow's Fast-Isaiah 58:7, I Kings 17:16 (NIV)

---

[44] NIV Life Application Study Bible. Copyright by Zondervan, Grand Rapids, Michigan, and co-published by Tyndale House Publishers, Inc. Carol Stream, Illinois. 2011.

Call for The Fasting Prayer

6. The Saint Paul Fast-*Isaiah* 58:8, Acts 9:9 (KJV)
7. The Daniel Fast- *Isaiah* 58:8, *Daniel* 1:8 (KJV)
8. The John the Baptist Fast-*Isaiah* 58:8. *Luke* 1:15 (KJV)
9. The Esther Fast-*Isaiah* 58:8, *Esther* 4:16, 5:2 (KJV) [45]

According to Jentezen Franklin in his book, *Fasting*, we find this definition of Biblical fasting, "Fasting is not merely going without food for some time. This is dieting and starving, but not fasting." [46]He continues to say fasting is not only done by ministers, monks, or fanatics. Franklin says fasting is refraining from food for a spiritual purpose and has always been a normal part of a relationship with God. Franklin gives one example of David fasting in *Psalm* 42:7, "*Deep calls unto deep.*" Franklin reminds us that as we fast from food from our usual diet for several days, our spirit

---
[45] Goll.
[46] Jentezen Franklin, *Fasting*, Charisma House, A Strang Company, 600 Rinehart Road, Lake Mary, Florida 32746, www.charismahouse.com. 9

Call for The Fasting Prayer

becomes uncluttered by the things of this world and sensitive with awareness to the things of our God. Franklin states that as David fasted, we too can begin to cry out from the depths of our spirit to the depths of God; even amid trials, our perspective will change. According to Franklin, fasting will soon become a secret source of power that many often overlook.[47] As I was writing about the Scriptures, thinking of our desires for food and fasting, I was reminded of Hosea 4:6 NKJV: *"My people are destroyed for lack of knowledge. Because you have rejected knowledge, I will also reject you from being priests for Me; because you have forgotten the law of your God, I will also forget your children."*[48]

---

[47] Franklin., 9-10.
[48] NKJV., https://www.bible.com. Hosea 4:6. NKJV

WHO CAN CALL A FAST?

The Almighty God can call you and me to a fasting prayer anytime. It is found in the Bible that the laity or clergy call fasts at various times. Daniel (laity), in *Daniel 1*, called for a fast for him and the Hebrew boys. In *Esther 4* (laity), Esther called for a fast, and Ana (laity) in the New Testament called for a fast. The prophet Joel (clergy), in *Joel 1:14*, called for a fast. After Jesus was led into the wilderness, God moved on Jesus to fast forty days and forty nights before He began His public ministry in *Matthew chapter* 4. These are just a few that called and entered prayer and fasting.

THE PURPOSE OF FASTING

Jentezen Franklin enlightened me about some of the purposes of fasting through his book, *Fasting*, which is "opening the door to a deeper, more intimate, more powerful relationship with God."[49] I began fasting before listening to and reading the book. The first Scripture in the book is *Matthew 5:6, "Blessed are those who hunger and thirst for righteousness, for they shall be filled."* This Scripture gives a higher purpose for denying food and liquids for such a time. *Mark 9:29*, KJV asks us for this kind of representative of the discipline of fasting. However, this was a book. Once I started reading it, I knew I had to buy more books and share them with others. According to Franklin, fasting is described as a secret to obtaining open doors, miraculous provision, favor, and a tender touch of God upon his life.[50] Franklin testifies that fasting is becoming a lifestyle. He continues with the purpose of fasting, which arises when one is growing dry spiritually, when one does not feel the innovative anointing, or when a fresh

---

[49] Franklin.
[50] Ibid.

encounter with the Almighty God is needed. Franklin states fasting is the secret key that unlocks Heaven's door, and slams shut the gates of hell. He goes on to explain in his book that there needs to be a desire for more than food and drink in the life of a Christian. He encourages the purpose of fasting, which is when there is a desperation to seek God in times when one needs answers, bondages to be broken, sickness and disease, and conditions, situations, and circumstances are impossible. Franklin reminds us of the following Scriptures:

- *Matthew 6: 1-18 NASU.* These Scriptures give evidence of a pattern for us to live purposefully as children of the Most High God. According to Franklin, the pattern is addressed in three specific duties of a Christian: giving, praying, and fasting. Franklin explains that Jesus clarified that fasting, giving, and praying were a regular part of a Christian life.

- *Ecclesiastes 4:12.* Franklin stated that when Solomon was writing the books of wisdom for Israel, the point was made that a cord or rope braided with three strands was not easily broken. Therefore, when giving, praying, and fasting are practiced together in a believer's life, it creates a three-fold cord that is not easily broken.[51]

OLD TESTAMENT FASTING DETAILS

Unless otherwise noted, the Scripture quotations are from the King James Version of the Bible.

Leviticus 23: 27-28: Israelites were called to a fast on the annual Day of Atonement. This fast represents a means of humbling oneself and repenting before God to seek Divine Forgiveness of sins.[52]

Exodus 34:28; Deuteronomy 9:9-10: This fast was a fast of Moses. Moses fasted from food and water for 80 days, in increments of two consecutive 40 days. This fast occurred on Mt.

---

[51] Franklin,10-11.
[52] Thomas A. Tarrants, "The Place of Fasting in the Christian Life," *Knowing and Doing, Knowing & Doing*, (June 6, 2018), https://www.cslewisinstitiute.org.

Call for The Fasting Prayer

Sinai during the great revelation meeting with the Almighty God.[53]

Daniel 10: Daniel observed this fast for twenty-one days. God gave Daniel important insight into Israel's future.[54]

1 *Samuel* 1:1-20: The story of Hannah. Hannah was barren, suffered from a broken heart, and was in a dangerously depressed state of mind for a child. Hannah persistently sought the Most High God in prayer and fasting. Her answer came through the birth of Samuel, who is known as one of the most outstanding leaders of the Old Testament.[55]

Ezra 8: 21-23: Ezra was exiled in Persia. While there, the king commissioned him to help restore Israel and proper worship of God. Ezra called for a fast among the Jewish exiles. The fast was to seek God in prayer and fasting for all travelers' safety, protection, and clearance for the journey back to Israel. God provided the answer.[56]

Nehemiah 1:1- 2:8: Nehemiah, while in exile, toiled with grief and concern for Israel and Jerusalem's conditions. Through fasting and praying, the Almighty God rendered favor to

---
[53] Tarrants.,
[54] Ibid.
[55] Ibid.
[56] Ibid.

Call for The Fasting Prayer

him with the king with a commission answer to return to Jerusalem. Nehemiah returned and rebuilt the city's walls with help from the people.[57]

Esther 4:16: God answered Esther's corporate prayers and fasting with the Jews. The prayer and fasting came at a time of impending doom among her people, and Esther was positioned to be instrumental in pleading for the whole nation.[58]

2 *Chronicles* 20:3: After a fast, God supplied deliverance for King Jehoshaphat and the people of Judah. King Jehoshaphat stood in the gap for Judah when he "set his face to seek the Lord and proclaim a fast throughout all Judah.[59]

Jonah 3: In the interim of Ninevah's prayer, fasting, and repentance, God was moved to answer for positive change.[60]

---

[57] Tarrants.
[58] Ibid.
[59] Ibid.
[60] Ibid.

NEW TESTAMENT FASTING DETAILS

Unless otherwise noted, the Scriptures referenced are from the King James Version of the Bible.

Luke 2:37: In the New Testament, fasting remains significant in the church's life, and many individuals believe and know it. The prophetess Anna, who "did not depart from the temple, worshiping with fasting and prayer night and day," gave a prophetic word to the parents of Jesus.[61]

Matthew 4:1-11: Jesus fasted for forty days in preparation for His public ministry. Scripture gives evidence of the outcome of this fasting, which Jesus endured as He faced the devil's temptations. [62]

Matthew 6: 5-6, Matthew 6: 16-18, Matthew 9: 14-15: Jesus' followers were expected to fast with proper motives, and the Almighty God would see and reward them accordingly. The same remains true of the rewards of prayer from a pure heart.[63]

---

[61] Tarrants.
[62] Ibid.
[63] Ibid.

Call for The Fasting Prayer

Acts 9:1-19: Saul of Tarsus fasted for three days after being blinded on the road of Damascus. When the fast was complete, Ananias, commissioned by Jesus, went to Saul to pray for him to recover his sight, be baptized, and be filled with the Holy Spirit. Saul also received his new name as Paul in Acts 13.[64]

Acts 13:1-2, Acts 14:23: In launching the first missionary journey in the church's history, fasting was an essential element in leading Saul (Paul), and Barnabas along with three other friends in the church at Antioch. Acts 13 speaks to the worshiping and fasting of the Lord. Then the Holy Spirit said, "Set apart for me Barnabas and Saul for the work to which I have called them." The work was fasting, praying, evangelism, and church planting. The church planting journey consisted of establishing churches and appointing elders by fasting and praying.[65]

THE CHURCH HISTORY OF PRAYER AND FASTING

Fasting and prayer did not just start in this century. According to James W. Goll, fasting

---

[64] Tarrants.
[65] Ibid.

Call for The Fasting Prayer

began in the Bible with Moses. The discipline of fasting in Scripture was the 40-day fast of Moses when God met with him on Mount Sinai (*Exodus 34:28; Deuteronomy 9:9*). The second 40-day fast (*Deuteronomy 9:18*) was when the tablets of stone were replaced.[66] Goll gives accounts of early church history through the following:

- Epiphanius, Bishop of Salamis, was born in 315 A.D. Early church history noted that Christians began fasting twice weekly, choosing Wednesdays and Fridays to avoid being confused with Pharisees, who fasted Tuesdays and Thursdays. Epiphanius stated, "Who does not know that the fast of the fourth and sixth days of the week is observed by Christians worldwide?"

- In Preparation of Special "Holy Days" - The practice of fasting for several days before the pagan holiday referred to by many as Easter was to prepare spiritually for the celebration of the resurrection of Jesus. Later, this was established as a time of special seeking

---

[66] Goll.

of the face of God during the Lent 40-day period before Easter. Partial fasting was usually observed. Fasting was encouraged in the second and third centuries of the church as preparation for water baptism.

- Fasting in Revival Movements- Fasting has long been associated with reforms and revivalistic movements throughout the church's history. The founders of the monastic movements practiced fasting as a regular part of their lifestyles. Each of the 16th-century reformers (and those earlier) also practiced fasting, as did the leaders of the evangelical great awakenings. John Wesley (founder of Methodism) would not ordain clergy to ministry unless they fasted two days every week. Johnathan Edwards was known to have fasted before God before releasing his famous message "Sinners in Hands of an Angry God." Goll also stated that during the Layman's Prayer Revival in North America in 1859, Christians fasted during their lunch hours and attended prayer meetings.

- Charles Finney noted revivalists would retreat and fast if they felt the anointing lift off their lives and preach until the spirit returned.

Call for The Fasting Prayer

- Pharisees- Fasted Tuesdays and Thursdays of each week, it is believed. (*Luke* 18:11-12)

- Jesus Christ- An extended fast of 40 days and 40 nights before beginning His public ministry (Mark 4:1-11). Jesus observed fasting as part of His heritage through the yearly Jewish fast called the Day of Atonement. Jesus taught fasting according to *Matthew* 6:16-18 to the disciples.[67]

THE BEGINNING OF MY FASTING LIFESTYLE

I was in my twenties the first time that I fasted and prayed. The first time my pastor asked us to pray and fast was only on Saturdays until noon. I remember I would give up Cokes during this fast and prayer time. This fast was a huge challenge for me. I loved Cokes. I would drink a Coke for breakfast, lunch, and dinner. So, fasting until noon on Saturday meant I had to give up two Cokes a day. We did this fast for

---
[67] Goll.

Call for The Fasting Prayer

one month only on Saturday till noon. Each Sunday, we would be accountable and stand if we had fasted the day before.

Few would stand in the beginning. As time went on, the congregation responded with more participation. I was not yet praying the Scripture in my prayers. Prayer and fasting are my lifeline now and have been for many years. Why do I say these Spiritual Disciplines of prayer and fasting are lifelines to me? I am glad you asked. As a young woman in my twenties, and a member of a beautiful Baptist Church led by a dynamic preacher of the Living God who taught the Word of God on Wednesday nights and Sundays faithfully, my journey started with living a fasted lifestyle through prayer. I have many testimonies of prayer and fasting during my lifetime. I have become a better person serving the Lord since I pray and fast continuously. I usually pray and fast privately. There are times when I do ask

Call for The Fasting Prayer

others to join me in prayer and fasting. However, I have learned to discern the people who I request to join me. I have seen much growth throughout the years of reading, studying, praying, and fasting with others.

My fasting testimonies are real. I recall a powerful sermon leading into the Lenten Season of 40 days to Easter Sunday, which represents Resurrection Sunday to some in Christendom. My pastor asked the congregation to fast and pray. I do not believe this was ever asked of us before this particular Sunday service. Pastor Jones went on to explain fasting to us from the book of Daniel, explaining Daniel's prayer and fasting journey. He told us about giving up some food(s) or drink (s) we loved for the 40 days, not just half a day once a week. Pastor Jones was stretching us to grow in the Lord. He explained it would be a considerable sacrifice, but it still would not measure up to the sacrifice of Jesus giving His life for us on the cross. My pastor asked the congregation to join him in the fast; I began to pray so I could hear from the Holy Spirit as to what sacrificial offering I was to give up during the fast.

As I prayed it was revealed to me just what foods I would give up for the fast. One of my favorite foods that I eat almost daily is cornbread. I love cornbread. Whether cooked on top of the stove in a skillet or baked in the oven, it does not matter. I love it. I love bread. So, when we would go to our favorite restaurants, such as Luby's or Red Lobster, my challenge was not to eat the cornbread muffins or the delicious cheese biscuits. My family knew I was determined not to eat the bread for the 40 days of the Lenten Season. They would chime in and say "Oh, the cornbread muffins or the cheese biscuits are so warm and tasty, but remember, you cannot have any." I would simply say "I know, and it is

Call for The Fasting Prayer

okay." If you just give up food and or drinks, then you are just dieting. The key is to pray and give up sacrificial foods and or beverages. If we just give up food and drinks, such as for a medical fast before having blood work, and do not pray, we should not expect or experience anything from God.

My prayer and fasting journey began with a desire. Prayer and fasting can take on a new meaning when seeking the face of God for answered prayer. When we find the desire to begin after hearing or studying the word of God concerning fasting and prayer, then the capacity springs forth for you and me to begin a wonderful journey. Often, so many people seem to think that they know all there is to know about praying, and that it does not take all *that* to get a prayer through to God. For some of us, staying connected and hearing from God does take all that and more. I am praying for every reader of this anthology to

Call for The Fasting Prayer

have a stirring up of desire and that they will pray for others to have the same desire to know and please El Shaddi in the Name of Jesus. Through my dedicated prayers and fasting, I have become an intercessor for the Most High God (*Psalm* 92). I am grateful to be used in the army of the Lord.

A significant time of fasting and praying took place in 2002 in my life. I could no longer escape my calling to preach the Gospel of Jesus Christ—a long story comprised to make it a short testimony. In 2002, I experienced many new things in my walk with God. The year began with significant change during a prayer retreat in January. By September of that year, I accepted my calling as a preacher of the Living God. At the time, I was attending a church where my nephew was the pastor, but I was still unsure about my calling into ministry.

Call for The Fasting Prayer

By November, I heard the call again—this time during a Sunday service. The call was clear: I was to go forward to the altar and publicly acknowledge my calling into ministry. However, I allowed myself to be distracted by my husband, and I missed my moment. The atmosphere in the service shifted, and the time for going to the altar passed. I felt deep conviction and repented at the altar after the service, knowing that I needed to proclaim my acceptance of God's calling on my life.

Following this experience, I embarked on a three-day fast and prayer vigil. I spent those days in isolation, fasting completely from solid food and consuming only liquids. I secluded myself in my upstairs office, sitting on the floor and immersing myself in God's Word. I studied passages about healing and deliverance, recording myself as I read the Bible and captured the words of wisdom God

Call for The Fasting Prayer

revealed to me during this intense time of prayer and study.

This fast was unlike anything I had experienced before. God instructed me to not only fast but also isolate myself. I could not talk on the phone or have casual conversations with anyone, not even my husband or my daughters. While my husband was allowed to remain in the house, I could only speak to him when absolutely necessary. This isolation was challenging, especially because my husband often cooked breakfast for us. On the first day of the fast, the aroma of bacon and toast filled the house, testing my resolve. I had to go downstairs, see the food, and remind him that I could only have liquids.

The hardest part of the fast was not speaking to my two daughters for three days and nights. It required discipline and focus, but I understood that this fast was about giving

Call for The Fasting Prayer

God the glory for choosing me to carry and deliver His Word. By the end of those three days, I emerged changed. This experience marked the beginning of my ministry, and I have carried the lessons from that time with me ever since.

Another period of fasting took place in 2021. I began a 30-day fast originally of not eating breakfast meats and then I heard God calling me to start a new fast of greater intensity without bread or breakfast meats. I was unsure how long the fast would be, but I started with 30 days, then it went to 40 days, then 90 days; the fast continued through the Lenten season, I could not stop fasting because I had so much going on in my life and my family's life at that time. I needed change to take place in my life. My family needed a change to happen. I needed to write and complete at least one book before the summer of 2021 ended. My youngest daughter Jaime

Call for The Fasting Prayer

was working on her first children's book about her daughter, "Harmony, and her best friend, Rex." I was taken by surprise and was asked to edit her book. My name was included in the book as an editor. This was the beginning of my name being in a book. It was not as the main author but as an editor of the book. I had given input to the story through editing. While still on this continuous fast, I began to gather my material on the various subjects I had written about throughout the last 20 years. Glory to God for the excellent press in the Spirit.

In 2022, after completing a year-long fast of giving up breakfast meats and bread—foods I dearly love, such as pork bacon, beef sausage, and all kinds of bread—I experienced a breakthrough. During this time, I completed and published a journal on peace, titled 40 *Days of Prayer for Peace Journal*. The journal

Call for The Fasting Prayer

was released in February 2022, marking a significant milestone in my spiritual journey.

The journey to this journal was foreshadowed by events in the Fall of 2018, while I was pastoring a church in Manassa, Georgia. At that time, God reunited me with a ministry I had previously undertaken—sending out daily inspirational text messages. This time, however, the focus was on peace. Initially, I planned to send messages for 21 days, but as I neared the 21st day, God instructed me to continue for 30 days. When I reached 30 days, God spoke again: "My people need your encouragement." He pressed me to extend the messages to 50 days, sharing peace Scriptures daily.

After completing 50 days of peace-focused text messages, God said, "Now you can change to healing for the people." This season of ministry became a journey of fasting, praying,

Call for The Fasting Prayer

listening, and obeying. Through it, God reminded me of the unfinished manuscripts I had accumulated over more than 20 years. He brought to mind the many times a friend and I had worked together, encouraging each other to write and set goals to complete just one of our books—but to no avail.

This time, however, was different. After devoting myself to prayer and listening closely to God's direction, I committed to a fast without giving up. With God's guidance and discipline, I successfully completed the journal and continued fasting and praying until its publication. The result was the victory of seeing my work released to the world: 40 *Days of Prayer for Peace Journal*. To God be the glory! Hallelujah!

I can vividly remember a time when I was praying and fasting, seeking God's guidance to change jobs. I asked a friend and my sister to

Call for The Fasting Prayer

join me in fasting. Neither of them was accustomed to fasting or giving up anything for Jesus, but they agreed to join me. We committed to fasting for 30 days together, as each of us needed breakthroughs and changes in our lives. Throughout the fast, both my sister and my friend struggled. They wanted to quit and failed multiple times along the way. However, the God within me encouraged them to remain steadfast and resilient in the Lord. We had all grown up in the church, attending the same services and hearing the same messages about fasting, yet it was evident that we all grow and grasp spiritual truths at different rates and in different ways. None of us learn at the same time or in the same manner, but that's part of the beauty of our faith journey. I kept my promise to them, encouraging and supporting them through the fast because I knew from the start that it would be a challenge. It was an opportunity to stretch ourselves spiritually and reach the next level of faith. While they completed their 30-day fast, I continued on for 90 days. To God be the glory! Hallelujah! That experience not only strengthened us as individuals but also showed us the power of corporate fasting. It stretched me spiritually, proving that I could go beyond what I thought was possible, and it taught me to trust God in new ways. This took place over 20 years ago, but the lessons remain fresh in my heart. It serves as a reminder that we do not grow at the same rate physically or spiritually. Yet, as long as we remain faithful and thank God for every victory, no matter the pace, He will take us to the next level. Hallelujah!

A CALL TO ACTION

Fasting has the power to lead you into your destiny, align you with God's plans for your life, sharpen your spirituality, and transform mediocrity into excellence for God. But will fasting alone change things? No, fasting by itself is not enough. Prayer and fasting must be united to foster growth in the things of God.

If you stumble during a fast—perhaps missing a day or two—do not be discouraged. It is okay. Start again and keep pressing forward until you achieve victory for God in the name of Jesus. The journey is about perseverance and faithfulness, not perfection.

This chapter has covered much about prayer and fasting, yet it is only the beginning. There is so much more to explore and learn. My prayer is that this chapter has stirred within you a desire to seek the face of God in a deeper dimension of faith and trust. I encourage you to begin incorporating prayer and fasting into your life. I believe fasting and prayer should become a lifestyle for us as Believers. Whether it is a one-day fast or a 90-

day fast, private or corporate, fasting helps us become spiritually uncluttered. When I speak of being uncluttered, I mean that fasting allows us to prioritize our thoughts and actions in a way that pleases God. It creates space for us to hear God's voice clearly and respond to His guidance quickly. For some, this chapter may lead you into uncharted waters with God but take heart—God is with you every step of the way. In *Isaiah* 43:2, God promises that we will not be consumed because He is with us. I pray that someone reading this chapter feels compelled to begin fasting and praying. Remember, you do not have to wait for a pastor or preacher to call a fast. The Most High God, Elohim, El Shaddai, will direct you to fast if you are listening and willing to obey. Amen.

Call for The Fasting Prayer

A PRAYER FOR YOU

Spirit of the Living God, thank You for falling fresh on Your people as they read this chapter and seek to draw nearer to You in spirit and truth. Eternal One, we are grateful for the desire You have placed within us to deny ourselves through prayer and fasting for Your glory. Lord, awaken within us a deeper longing for Your presence, a hunger that surpasses all else. Teach us the purpose and power of fasting, that we may quiet our minds, surrender our flesh, and make room for Your voice.

Father, thank You for comforting us in our physical bodies when the flesh craves food or when distractions arise, and for giving us strength to stay committed to the sacred practice of fasting and prayer. Forgive us, Lord, when we stumble on this journey, and thank You for Your grace that allows us to start again, learning from the examples of faith found in Your Word.

Guide us, Lord Jesus, in this journey of fasting and prayer, giving us courage, discipline, and steadfast hearts. Let this time be one of growth, healing, and revelation. May we find joy in communing with You, and may our lives be testimonies of Your grace, love, and power. Draw us closer to You, Lord, and let all we do honor Your holy name.

Call for The Fasting Prayer

In the Name of Jesus, we pray, Amen.

BIBLIOGRAPHY

Goll, James W., "Consecrated, Contemplative Prayer-The Fasted Life," https://itsallaboutyeshua.wordpress.com/2013/09/24/consecrated-contemplative-prayer-the-fasted-life-by-james-w-goll/

Franklin, Jentezen. Fasting, Charisma House, A Strang Company, 600 Rinehart Road, Lake Mary, Florida 32746. www.charismahouse.com.

King James Version Bible

Logos, Phil. "How many times is prayer mentioned in the Bible."https://bibletrivia.co.uk/trivia/how-many-times-is-prayer-mentioned-in-the-bible.

McKim, Donald K., "Westminster Dictionary of Theological Terms," Westminster John Knox Press, Louisville, Kentucky, 1996, 1st Ed.102.

NKJV., https://www.bible.com>Hosea 4:6. NKJV

NIV Life Application Study Bible. Copyright by Zondervan, Grand Rapids, Michigan and co-published by Tyndale House Publishers, Inc. Carol Stream, Illinois.2011.2348.

Study.com

Tarrants, Thomas A., "The Place of Fasting in the Christian Life, "Knowing *and Doing, Knowing & Doing*, (June 6, 2018).
https://www.cslewisinstitute.org.

The BibleStudyTools Staff on 1.15.24.
https://www.biblestudytools.com/tropical-verses/bible-verses-about-fasting

ABOUT THE CONTRIBUTOR

Dr. Rhonda Y. Green Harmon, author of 40 Days of Prayer for PEACE Journal, is an Ordained Elder and serves as the pastor of Historic Payne Chapel AME Church in Brunswick, Georgia. She is married to Exhorter A.J. Harmon and is the proud mother of two daughters and grandmother to one granddaughter. A graduate of Texas Southern University, the University of Houston, Houston Graduate School of Theology, and Southern Methodist University, Dr. Harmon has received numerous honors throughout her academic journey. She founded Rhonda Green Harmon Circle of Life Ministries, a non-profit organization, and is known as a "Wordologist" and "Prayerologist." Dr. Harmon leads the Staying Connected to the Vine Prayer and Bible Study Call and is active on social media through Rhonda Green Harmon Ministries. A servant leader, she conducts prayer retreats, Bible studies, and offers mentorship across global cultural lines. Pastor Rhonda's healing ministry brings love, peace, and restoration, making her a beloved spiritual leader to many.

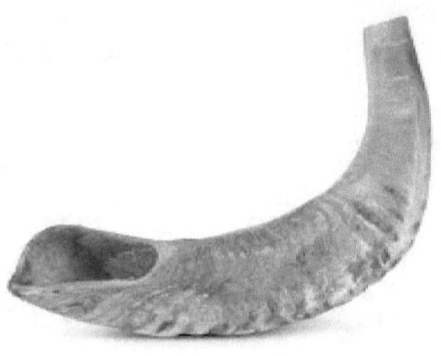

4

CALL FOR THE WAILING WOMEN

Dr. Tammy Isaac

At the time that Jeremiah was called to be a prophet it was not at a time of great joy. The nation was on the decline. "When he was called, it was intimated to Jeremiah that his message would be one of condemnation

Call for The Wailing Women

rather than salvation." [68]. His preaching theme would be one of judgment

> to a traumatized world—[who's] inhabitants [are] facing the cataclysmic crisis of their world come[ing] undone. Around 597 BCE, the people of Judah experienced the terrifying invasion of their country by the Babylonian army led by Nebuchadnezzar, which then forcefully removed a large number of people into exile. A decade later, a second round of attacks (587 BCE) destroyed the city and temple and ended with the people of Judah further exiled to far-away Babylon. From the depths of these anguished times, we witness in the book of Jeremiah the first raw poetic expressions of people seeking to come to terms with the terror around them.[69]

---

[68] J. D. Douglas and Merrill C. Tenney, Zondervan's Pictorial Bible Dictionary, Supersaver ed. (Maplewood, N.J.: Zondervan, 1999)

[69] L Juliana M. Claassens. 2010. "Calling the keeners: the image of the wailing woman as symbol of survival in a traumatized world." Journal Of Feminist Studies In Religion 26, no. 1: 63-77. ATLA Religion Database with ATLASerials, EBSCOhost (accessed June 13, 2013).

Call for The Wailing Women

Jeremiah was to inform the people of Israel of the impending death that was coming their way because of their continuous sin against God. Jeremiah "is calling on a people facing imminent destruction to repent of their idolatry and injustice and accept the punishment God is about to bring."[70] He tells them to *"Consider now! Call for the wailing (mourning) women to come; send for the most skillful of them. Let them come quickly and wail over us till our eyes overflow with tears and water streams from our eyelids"*, Jeremiah 9:17, 18 (NIV). The prophet Jeremiah's call for the wailing women is not a mere cultural footnote of ancient Israel but a profound spiritual practice that speaks volumes to our present age. Mourning (wailing) is an invitation for God's presence to intersect with our pain. It is both a cry of the soul and a call to action, beckoning all who hear to engage deeply with

---
[70] "Grace Community Fellowship," The Grace Institute, June 13, 2013, accessed June 13, 2013, http://www.gcfweb.org/institute/prophet/jeremiah-1.html.

the weight of loss and the urgency of intercession. Through Jeremiah, God calls upon the wailing women to lead the community in mourning, demonstrating that grief is a communal experience. In this chapter, we will explore the role of the wailing women, the power of mourning, and the timeless application of these practices in our contemporary lives.

WHAT IS MOURNING?

Wailing, lament, and mourning are interconnected yet distinct aspects of grief and loss. Wailing is the vocal expression of intense sorrow or grief, often characterized by loud cries, sobs, or moaning. It serves as a spontaneous or ritualized release of the emotional burden of grief.

> The word "wail" originated in the Middle English period, around 1300-50. It may come from the Old English

Call for The Wailing Women

word weilāwei wellaway or the Old English word wǣlan, which means "to torment"[71]

In many cultures and traditions, wailing is an immediate and visceral reaction to loss, providing a powerful way to externalize inner anguish. Wailing is often a component of both mourning and lament, functioning as a personal and communal acknowledgment of sorrow.

Lament, on the other hand, is a structured expression of grief, pain, or regret, often directed toward God or a higher power. It takes the form of prayer, poetry, or song and goes beyond mere emotional expression. Lament seeks to engage with God, inviting His presence into the sorrow and pleading for His intervention, healing, or justice. While lament often includes wailing, it incorporates

---

[71] "Wail," Online Etymology Dictionary, accessed December 28, 2024, https://www.etymonline.com/word/wail.

intentional reflection, theology, and hope. Unlike the raw instinctiveness of wailing, lament is purposeful, offering a pathway through grief and seeking transformation. It can be both personal and communal, depending on its context.

Mourning is the overall process of responding to loss, encompassing both internal emotions and outward expressions of grief. It allows individuals and communities to process their loss, commemorate the deceased, and adapt to a changed reality. Wailing and lament frequently play significant roles in mourning. Wailing may occur as an immediate, raw reaction within the broader context of mourning, while lament offers a reflective and spiritual approach to the grieving process.

> The word mourn came . . . from Old English, from the word *murnan*, which meant to bemoan, to long after, or to be anxious about. *Murnan* came from a

Call for The Wailing Women

Proto-Germanic word of the same spelling, which meant to remember sorrowfully, and which likely came from the Proto-Indo-European root, (s)*mer-*, meaning to remember.[72]

Mourning is the outward expression of grief that typically accompanies the loss of someone or something deeply significant, such as a loved one, a way of life, or a community tragedy. It is a natural, emotional, and often ritualistic response to the experience of loss. When experiencing the emotions of grief, one is destined to mourn. "When death is mentioned in the bible frequently it relates to the experience of the bereaved, which will normally respond immediately, outwardly, and without reserve."[73] Weeping was then as it is now the

---

[72] Suzanne Purkis, "The Etymology of Death, Grief, and Mourning," *Apoplectic Apostrophes: Confessions of a Grammar Ghoul* (December 3, 2015), accessed July 5, 2020, https://lucidedit.wordpress.com/2015/12/03/the-etomology-of-death-grief-and-mourning/.

[73] Charles W. Draper, Chad Brand, and Archie England, eds., Holman Illustrated Bible Dictionary, Revised ed. (Chattanooga: Holman Reference, 2003).

Call for The Wailing Women

primary indication of grief with tears and loud wailing. Mourning is about taking "the grief you have on the inside and expressing it outside yourself. Another way of defining mourning is 'grief gone public' or 'the outward expression of grief.'"[74] How one mourns reflects one's cultural customs. "Mourning was considered among Jews to be honorable and necessary."[75] Every culture has specific ways in which to express grief.

> Rabbinic traditions reflected in the Talmud also demonstrate that mourning was an important obligation and one which aroused considerable debate as to the proprieties of the rituals. So important was the obligation to mourn that performing the meth mizwah24 took precedence over the study of Torah (if there are insufficient numbers to bury the dead)

---

[74] Allen Wolfelt, "Grief", "Grief?' Center for Loss and Life Transition. Accessed March 8, 2019, http://www.centerforloss.com/grief/.

[75] Rick Strelan, "To Sit Is to Mourn: The Women at the Tomb (Matthew 27:61)," *Colloquium* 31, no. 1 (May 1999): 31–45, accessed October 12, 2019, http://search.ebscohost.com/login.aspx?direct=true&db=rfh&AN=A TLA0000987780&site=ehost-live.

and to a Temple service (Meg. 3b, 29a). So, in the matter of mourning, the Master said: "Great is the obligation to pay due respect to human beings, since it overrides a negative precept of the Torah" (Meg. 3b). Even the poorest was to have a professional female mourner and two flautists (M. Ket. 4.4); and Deut 21:22-23 already made it obligatory that those crucified be properly buried.[76]

There is no one right or only way to mourn. Talking about the person who died, crying, expressing thoughts and feelings through art or music, journaling, praying, and celebrating special anniversary dates that held meaning for the person who died are just a few examples of mourning. Other ways mourning was expressed in the Bible were by the tearing of clothes (Gen. 37:34), the removal of sandals to walk barefoot (2 Sam. 15:30), the throwing of dust on the head (Josh. 7:6; 1 Sam. 4:12; 2 Sam. 1:2; 13:19; Neh. 9:1), and/or the covering

---

[76] Strelan.

of the head (Esth. 6:12; Jer. 14:4). Some would pull out their own hair (Ezra 9:3) as a sign of emotional distress. Brand offers, "They might refrain from washing and other normal activities (2 Sam. 3:31) . . .. Women wore black or somber material (2 Sam. 14:2)."[77] Men wore sackcloth and ashes, which Knight details, "This material was woven from goat and camel hair or some other rough fiber such as hemp. The discomfort associated with wearing clothes made of such rough cloth symbolized the anguish and turmoil of those who had lost loved ones. See also 1 Kings 21:17-27; 2 Kings 19:1; Esth. 4:1; Job 16:15; Jon. 3:5."[78]

The connection between wailing, lament, and mourning is evident in how they overlap and complement one another. Wailing is often the instinctive cry of anguish that initiates

---

[77] Brand, Draper, and England. 691.
[78] George W. Knight, *The Illustrated Guide to Bible Customs and Curiosities* (Uhrichsville, OH: Barbour Publications, 2007).

mourning, while lament channels grief into purposeful prayer or reflection. Mourning, as a broader experience, provides the structure and space for both wailing and lament to unfold. Together, they create a holistic approach to processing loss, allowing individuals and communities to navigate the depths of sorrow while finding paths to healing and restoration.

Despite their interrelation, wailing, lament, and mourning differ in their nature and intent. Wailing is primarily emotional and physical, while lament is spiritual and reflective, often directed toward God. Mourning encompasses both and serves as a comprehensive process shaped by cultural and personal factors. Wailing is spontaneous, lament is deliberate, and mourning is structured. Each plays a vital role in helping individuals and communities engage with grief in meaningful ways.

Wailing, lament, and mourning are deeply interconnected expressions of grief that honor the complexity of human emotion. Wailing provides a raw outlet for sorrow, lament transforms grief into spiritual dialogue, and mourning creates a framework for these expressions to unfold and lead to healing. Together, they remind us of the importance of engaging with grief rather than suppressing it, allowing us to honor our losses and move toward God for restoration.

MOURNING AS A FORM OF PRAYER

Mourning acknowledges the brokenness of our world and directs our cries to the One who can heal and restore. Mourning wasn't just an indication of grief but also as a supplication, a prayer of petition, a prayer of intercession unto God.

Call for The Wailing Women

> Without the prayer of [mourning], the other important elements of prayer—praise, thanksgiving, confession, intercession—atrophy and ring hollow. How can praise be free and joyful if the realities of broken human life are not named and lamented? How can heartfelt thanks be given for healing if the wounds are denied? How can confession of sin be sincere if we turn all sor- row into guilt? How can intercession be strong if our language does not reflect knowledge of the real sufferings of those for whom we pray?[79]

The weeping of God's people invites God's heart to act on their behalf; *John 11:33 When Jesus saw her weeping, and the Jews who had come along with her also weeping, he was deeply moved in spirit and troubled.* When we wail, lament, and mourn, we welcome God into our circumstances. Our cries become a form of prayer, acknowledging His sovereignty and our dependence on Him.

---

[79] Ellen F. Davis, *Getting Involved with God: Rediscovering the Old Testament* (Lanham, MD: Cowley Publications, 2001).

Call for The Wailing Women

Through our wailing, lamenting, and mourning we express our trust in God's ability to bring comfort, justice, and restoration. The Psalms are rich with examples of wailing, lamenting, and mourning prayers that begin with anguish but often end in praise and hope, demonstrating that wailing, lamenting, and mourning is not a destination but a bridge to God's presence. These examples illustrate that such expressions of grief are not an endpoint but a bridge to God's presence:

> "I am worn out from my groaning. All night long I flood my bed with weeping and drench my couch with tears. My eyes grow weak with sorrow; they fail because of all my foes." Psalm 6:6-9 (NIV)

This psalm begins with the psalmist's cries of distress and physical exhaustion from sorrow. Yet, it transitions to hope and confidence as the psalmist declares in verse 9:"The Lord has heard my cry for mercy; the Lord accepts my prayer."

Call for The Wailing Women

*"How long, Lord? Will you forget me forever?
How long will you hide your face from me?"
Psalm 13:1-6 (NIV)*

Here, David begins with a desperate lament, expressing feelings of abandonment and despair. However, by the end of the psalm, his tone shifts to faith and praise: *"But I trust in your unfailing love; my heart rejoices in your salvation. I will sing the Lord's praise, for he has been good to me."*

*"My God, my God, why have you forsaken me?
Why are you so far from saving me, so far from my cries of anguish?" Psalm 22:1-5 (NIV)*

This psalm is a vivid expression of wailing and lament, famously echoed by Jesus on the cross. Yet, even in the depths of despair, the psalmist recalls God's faithfulness: *"In you our ancestors put their trust; they trusted, and you delivered them."*

Call for The Wailing Women

"My tears have been my food day and night, while people say to me all day long, 'Where is your God?'" Psalm 42:3-5 (NIV)

The psalmist describes profound mourning and spiritual turmoil but encourages himself to hope in God: *"Why, my soul, are you downcast? Why so disturbed within me? Put your hope in God, for I will yet praise him, my Savior and my God."*

"Have mercy on me, O God, according to your unfailing love; according to your great compassion blot out my transgressions." Psalm 51:1-12 (NIV)

This psalm is David's lament after his sin with Bathsheba, filled with deep mourning for his wrongdoing. Yet it is also a prayer for renewal and hope: *"Create in me a pure heart, O God, and renew a steadfast spirit within me."*

"I cried out to God for help; I cried out to God to hear me. When I was in distress, I sought

Call for The Wailing Women

the Lord; at night I stretched out untiring hands, and I would not be comforted."
Psalm 77:1-14 (NIV)

The psalmist begins in despair, questioning God's presence, but transitions to remembering God's mighty deeds: *"Your ways, God, are holy. What god is as great as our God? You are the God who performs miracles; you display your power among the peoples."*

These psalms reveal that wailing, lamenting, and mourning are part of a sacred journey—an honest expression of the human condition before God. They show us that grief is not the final word but a bridge to His presence, where anguish gives way to trust, hope, and ultimately, praise. Through these prayers, we learn that God welcomes our cries and meets us in our brokenness, transforming sorrow into a deeper connection with Him.

Call for The Wailing Women

TEARS AS AN EXPRESSION OF MOURNING

In a culture that often rushes to avoid pain or bypass grief, mourning stands as a countercultural practice that embraces the fullness of human emotion. One of the most popular ways of mourning is through weeping. As Lipton words it, "Tears, and sounds such as wailing and moaning, may thus represent either emotional or ritual responses."[80] Mourning gives one an avenue to seek the face of God to restore a broken heart (deep sorrow), although it does not necessarily change that there is a loss or tragedy. Weeping is a way of communicating one's deep sorrow. God hears the thoughts, concerns, and emotions of those who are in deep sorrow (grief) when they are unable to

---

[80] Diana Lipton, "Early Mourning? Petitionary Versus Posthumous Ritual in Ezekiel xxiv," *Vetus Testamentum* 56, no. 2 (2006): 185–202, accessed November 2, 2019, https://search.ebscohost.com/login.aspx?direct=true&db=rfh&AN=ATLA0001513137&site=ehost-live.

speak a word because of what they are experiencing at the time. "One of the best examples in Jeremiah of the community's response to its trauma is the tears cried by the keener or the wailing woman,"[81] according to Claassens, in her book, *Mourner, Mother, Midwife: Reimagining God's Delivering Presence in the Old Testament.*

Claassens suggests, "The wailing women's tears, which represent the depth of the community's emotion in the face of extreme trauma, are closely connected to the tears of God in Jer. 8:21–3; Matt. 8:21–9:1."[82] Jeremiah's grief reflects not only his own grief but also God's grief for his people. The pain of Jeremiah is the pain of God; thus, the tears of Jeremiah are the tears of God. "Jeremiah's sorrow is a mirroring of the grief of the

---

[81] L. Juliana M. Claassens, *Mourner, Mother, Midwife* (Minneapolis: Fortress Press, 2013), 26.
[82] Claassens, "Calling the Keeners.

Call for The Wailing Women

LORD."[83] Israel's rebellion brought God grief and it "provides the reasons for the tears of God and God's desire to escape to the wilderness."[84] The unfaithfulness of Israel brings out "divine empathy, vulnerability, and profound sorrow. Grief overtakes anger, sympathy replaces fury."[85]

Tears are an expression of what people feel at the time, and "only the weeping God can feel the people's pain; only the suffering God can help . . . a God who identifies with its pain."[86] Tears give voice to that which the traumatized are unable to speak. "The image of God who weeps offers an interruption that allows new possibilities for hope to emerge."[87] The Lord's tears for His people also give voice to His

---

[83] Claassens, "Calling the Keeners.
[84] Kathleen M. O'Connor, "The Tears of God and Divine Character in Jeremiah 2-9," in *God in the Fray: A Tribute to Walter Brueggemann*, Tod Linafelt and Timothy K. Beal, eds. (Minneapolis: Fortress Press, 1980, 172–185.
[85] O'Connor, *Jeremiah: Pain and Promise*.
[86] Ibid.
[87] Ibid.

Call for The Wailing Women

promise that He will still be their deliverer in times of judgement. Claassens notes,

> It is important to understand that the image of God who weeps is a product of a community that, through its tears, was seeking to come to terms with its communal and individual grief. The book of Jeremiah permeated with tears; heaven and earth mourn (Jer. 4:28), Rachel cries inconsolably for her children who are no more (Jer. 31:15-17), and, as we have seen before, the tears of the prophet merge with God's tears (Jer. 8:21-9:1; Matt. 8:21-23). It is indeed a traumatized and bereaved people who imagined their God as weeping.[88]

Abraham Heschel, in his book *The Prophets*, has a remarkable study on the pathos of God in which he clearly shows that the God of the Bible experiences emotions and suffers with and because of his people. "The wailing women's tears, which represent the depth of

---

[88] Claassens, "Calling the Keeners.

Call for The Wailing Women

the community's emotion in the face of extreme trauma, are closely connected to the tears of God . . . to the extent that we can say [that] God's tears are embodied in [the] wailing women,"[89] as found in Jeremiah 9. Rabbi Kalonymus Kalman Sharprio, quoted in Herbert J. Levine's, *Sing unto God a New Song: A Contemporary Reading of the Psalms*, expounds,

> The weeping, the pain that a person undergoes by himself, alone—they may have the effect of breaking him, of bringing him down, so that he is incapable of doing anything. But the weeping that the person does together with God—that strengthens him. . ... It is hard to rise, time and again, above the sufferings; but when one summons the courage—stretching the mind to engage in Torah and divine service—then he enters the inner chamber where God is to be found. There he

---

[89] Claassens, "Calling the Keeners.

Call for The Wailing Women

weeps and wails with Him, as it were together.⁹⁰

There is a song titled "Better Than A Hallelujah", sung by Amy Grant that talks about how God delights in the weeping of His people. This song offers a poignant reflection on the depth and honesty of human emotion, reminding us that God values our raw, unfiltered cries as much as—if not more than—our polished praises. The song echoes the message of this chapter: lament and mourning, even in their messiest and most vulnerable forms, are sacred to God. It reassures us that our tears, wailing, and broken prayers are not only heard by God but are cherished as expressions of genuine faith and trust.

God loves a lulluby
In a mother's tears in the dead of

---

⁹⁰ Rabbi Kalonymus Kalman Sharprio, quoted in Herbert J. Levine, *Sing Unto God a New Song: A Contemporary Reading of the Psalms* (Bloomington: Indiana University Press, 1995), 219.

Call for The Wailing Women

night
Better than a Hallelujah sometimes

God loves the drunkard's cry
The soldier's plea not to let him die
Better than a Hallelujah sometimes
We pour out our miseries
God just hears a melody
Beautiful, the mess we are
The honest cries of breaking hearts
Are better than a Hallelujah

The woman holding on for life
The dying man giving up the fight
Are better than a Hallelujah
sometimes

The tears of shame for what's been done
The silence when the words won't come
Are better than a Hallelujah
sometimes[91]

The lyrics, "The honest cries of breaking hearts are better than a hallelujah," capture the essence of how God invites us to bring our

---

[91] Amy Grant, "Better Than a Hallelujah," elyrics.net, June 13, 2013, accessed June 13, 2013, http://www.elyrics.net/read/a/amy-grant-lyrics/better-than-a-hallelujah-lyrics.html.

whole selves to Him, including our pain and sorrow. It emphasizes that lament is not a sign of weakness but a profound act of worship—an acknowledgment of our need for God's presence in the midst of suffering. Like the wailing women in Jeremiah, who cried out for their community's healing and restoration, the song invites us to embrace the power of vulnerable, heartfelt lament as a pathway to God's grace.

This song reminds us that God is not distant in our mourning; He is moved by it. Our grief and wailing become prayers that rise to Him, drawing His compassion and intervention. In this way, *Better Than a Hallelujah* serves as modern-day mourning, teaching us that in moments of profound brokenness, our honest cries create space for God to move, heal, and restore. It is a beautiful affirmation that even in our tears, we are seen, heard, and deeply loved by God.

THE ROLE OF WAILING WOMEN

Through the prophet God announces judgment on His people but not without reason. In verses 13 and 14, "The Lord said, "It is because they have forsaken my law, which I set before them; they have not obeyed me or followed my law. Instead, they have followed the stubbornness of their hearts; they have followed the Baals, as their ancestors taught them." The people had forsaken God's law, disobeyed His voice, and walked according to their own heart; spiritual and literal adultery, treachery and falsehood, deceit and slander, refusal to know God, and planning evil against people while hiding it behind friendly masks, and the Lord Almighty says in *Jeremiah 9:17-18 (NIV)*, *"Consider now! Call for the wailing (mourning) women to come; send for the most skillful of them. Let them come quickly and wail over us till our eyes overflow with tears and water streams from our eyelids.*

Call for The Wailing Women

"Yahweh begins addressing the people directly, telling them they had better think about calling the mourning (wailing) women to come and lead their laments."[92]

There was an urgency in the Lord's plea for the people to call for wailing women to come quickly. "The reason for the haste is that lamentations can already be heard in parts of the city where refugees from outlying areas are lamenting loss of land and homes."[93] The people of Israel needed the act of mourning to go on so that restoration would come to them. "Even in the face of the mighty Babylonian empire, and probably with little real power to change their situation, wailing women's tears became a way to resist the brutal devastation of the empire that has crushed everything in its way, by refusing to accept the current situation as it is . . . ."[94] "The image of the

---

[92] O'Connor, *Jeremiah: Pain and Promise*
[93] Claassens, "Calling the Keeners."
[94] Ibid.

Call for The Wailing Women

wailing women, as it occurs in the ancient text of Jeremiah, provides contemporary readers with intriguing possibilities for dealing with our own often fragile and flawed attempts in coming to terms with those situations where tragedy has struck on a personal and/or communal level."[95] The tears of the wailing women were an expression of what the people of Judah should have been feeling at that time. "Within the book's narrative world, the grief in these poems is anticipatory, stirred up before disaster to dramatize its coming destructiveness."[96] The message is one of hope, allowing readers the opportunity to turn to God and seek Him through prayer, an expression of mourning through the journey of grief.

---

[95] Claassens, "Calling the Keeners.
[96] O'Connor, *Jeremiah: Pain and Promise*.

THE SKILLED WAILING WOMEN WERE TAUGHT

The wailing women were "professional mourners who [were] especially skilled women urged to sing their laments as over the dead.... The most skillful of them are needed because of the huge loss."[97] Skilled wailing women were also known was wise women; "suggesting that the art of mourning publicly was a learned skill... wailing women not only had to be able to draw on the reservoir of laments handed down through the generations, but women skilled in the art of lamenting were also to adapt these laments to suit the particular needs of the current situation." [98]The wailing women in Jeremiah's time were not just ordinary mourners; they were skilled practitioners of lament, trained in the art of expressing grief in ways that moved

---

[97] Hetty Lalleman, Jeremiah and Lamentations. (Downers Grove, IL: IVP Academic, 2013)
[98] Claassens, "Calling the Keeners.

hearts and inspired communal participation. Their role required both emotional depth and technical skill, as their wailing and lamenting had a spiritual and cultural significance that extended beyond individual sorrow. These women were intentional about their craft, learning how to wail and lament in ways that could lead others into collective mourning and prayer.

The scripture also highlights the importance of teaching this sacred practice to the next generation. In *Jeremiah 9:20*, it says, *"Now, you women, hear the word of the Lord; open your ears to the words of His mouth. Teach your daughters how to wail; teach one another a lament."* This verse underscores the need to pass down the skills of wailing and lamenting to young girls, ensuring that the art of expressing grief and leading communal mourning would not be lost. The call to teach daughters to wail was not just a cultural instruction but a spiritual mandate, recognizing the power of wailing as a way to lead the community into prayer and to invite God's presence into their situations. In the same way, we should be teaching our children—both boys and girls—to wail, lament, and mourn. These practices are essential tools for responding to loss and tragedy with prayer and faith. By equipping our children with the ability to express grief and lead others in lament, we prepare them for their future roles as leaders within their communities. When tragedy arises, these children, having been taught the sacred practice of lament, will be ready to stand and lead people of all genders into unified prayer for God's intervention.

Passing down these skills ensures that the next generation understands the value of communal mourning and its transformative power. It reinforces the idea that lament is not only for times of personal sorrow but also a vital communal response in times of crisis. By teaching our children to wail, lament, and mourn, we are equipping them with a spiritual inheritance that enables them to be leaders in faith, compassion, and prayer, uniting their communities and inviting God's healing presence into moments of collective grief.

LEADING THE COMMUNITY IN MOURNING

"There is a clear connection between not serving and obeying God and relationships with others: when God is exchanged for other gods and His commandments are ignored, the whole framework of the covenant community falls down, and no-one can be trusted."[99] The wailing women were summoned during times of impending or realized loss, such as war, death, or national calamity. They played a vital role in the spiritual health of the community,

---

[99] Lalleman.

Call for The Wailing Women

recognizing that mourning was not a sign of weakness but a necessary pathway to healing. Though the people were capable of grieving on their own, public mourning "declares death's triumph, makes its reality undeniable and something to be mourned. Their keening and lamenting created an environment of sorrow and expressed the grief of the bereaved."[100] Their wailing was more than expressions of sorrow; they were prayers that sought to draw God's attention to their plight and invite His intervention.

Jeremiah's call to the wailing women was not just for their sake but for the entire community. These women were to lead the way, modeling vulnerability and spiritual dependence for others to follow. Their role reminds us that grief and mourning are not solitary endeavors but communal responsibilities. Wailing women were not just

---

[100] Claassens, "Calling the Keeners.

emotional responders; they were spiritual leaders. Their cries pierced the heavens, carrying the grief of the people to the throne of God. They embodied the collective sorrow of the nation and gave voice to the unspoken pain of individuals. These women were skilled in [wailing], knowing how to express the depth of their anguish in ways that moved hearts and brought communities together in mourning. These women were called upon to come and help "the community deal with the situation at hand... their laments truly represented a community response to trauma."[101] The wailing women were called in because the people were unable to mourn for themselves. They did not comprehend the coming judgment of God because the false prophets were declaring to them "peace, peace" (6:14; 8:11).

---

[101] Claassens, "Calling the Keeners."

Call for The Wailing Women

Wailing (mourning) was a communal activity. It was a call-and-response expression of mourning. The head wailer led the people into public grieving and mourning. The head wailer began the wail and then others responded. Those who wailed used instruments, songs, and dances along with their voices. Through mourning, one could deal with and come through the grief journey. Wailers played a therapeutic role in their communities by not allowing anyone to grieve alone. They displayed the sharing of one another's deep sorrow by mourning with them. Claassens says, "The communal act of weeping releases emotional pressure that weighs heavy on subjects."[102] This allowed for a sacred space within the community to be formed so that those who grieved could do so with permission, without humiliation, and together with their community.

---

[102] Claassens, Calling the Keeners.

Call for The Wailing Women

Mourning gives one the opportunity to seek the face of God in an effort to restore broken relationships with God, although it may not stop the impending punishment that is set before those who have disobeyed the will of God. "In light of all that transpired, the only appropriate response to the terror all around was to raise one's voice in weeping and wailing... this response offered an avenue to deal with grief that otherwise might be too overwhelming for individuals to bear alone...."[103]

The wailing women were not merely mourners but spiritual catalysts, called to lead their communities into a profound expression of grief and lament. Their purpose extended beyond their own cries—they were to wail, lament, and mourn until their cries moved the hearts of others, filling their eyes with tears. The wailing women influenced the prayers of

---

[103] Claassens. Mourner, Mother, Midwife.

the people, stirring them to join in the communal lament. Their role was to create an environment where sorrow could no longer be suppressed or ignored, compelling men, women, boys, and girls alike to confront the depth of their grief and engage in collective mourning. This powerful example debunks the myth that only women are to wail, lament, or mourn. While the wailing women are the initiators of wailing, their leadership challenges the misconception that mourning is gendered. Their leadership revealed that mourning is a universal human responsibility. Their leadership showed that wailing belongs to everyone and has the power to bring healing and unity in the face of tragedy. When the wailing women lifted their voices, their wailing became contagious, drawing the entire community—men, women, boys, and girls—into the prayer of wailing, mourning, and lament. The wailing women wailed over the people until their "eyes overflow[ed] with tears and water stream[ed] from [their] eyelids", (18). This collective response emphasized that grief and lament are communal acts, meant to unite people in shared sorrow and collective cries for God's intervention.

By leading others in mourning, the wailing women demonstrated that lament is not a solitary expression but a shared spiritual practice. Their leadership transformed the act of mourning into a communal prayer, breaking down barriers and inspiring the entire community to seek hope and restoration together.

In today's world, we often compartmentalize grief, leaving individuals to carry their pain alone. The wailing women challenges this norm, showing us the power of collective lament. When the community gathers to mourn, healing is magnified, and the weight of sorrow is shared. Every man, woman, boy, and girl is called to take part in this sacred act, following the lead of the wailing women as they guide the community toward God's comfort and restoration.

MORDERN DAY MOURNING

Though the practice of wailing may seem archaic, its principles are as relevant today as they were in Jeremiah's time. Modern expressions of lament can take many forms, from spoken prayers and songs to written words and silent vigils. The essence of wailing and mourning lies in their authenticity and openness before God. In moments of personal or collective tragedy, we are invited to engage in wailing, mourning, and lament. Whether we are grieving the loss of a loved one, mourning societal injustices, or grappling with personal struggles, wailing allows us to process our pain in God's presence. It is through this process that we find comfort, strength, and the courage to move forward.

A modern-day wailer could take many forms, as the concept of wailing is not limited to literal crying or mourning but extends to individuals or groups who express deep grief, lament, or emotional outcry in response to personal, communal, or societal pain. Here are a few examples:

Community Leaders and Clergy

Pastors, chaplains, or spiritual leaders who guide communities through mourning, whether after personal tragedies or larger disasters, fulfill the role of wailers. They lead public prayers, provide emotional and spiritual support, and encourage communities to grieve openly. Leaders who speak on behalf of the hurting or suffering within their congregations also embody this role.

Call for The Wailing Women

Artists and Musicians

Songwriters, poets, and visual artists often act as wailers by creating works that capture the depths of human sorrow and loss. For example, songs of lament, protest anthems, or art that reflects grief and tragedy can resonate deeply with people, offering both an outlet for collective pain and a call for change. Artists like Amy Grant or worship leaders who create songs of lament bring attention to emotional and spiritual struggles.

Advocates and Activists

Activists who raise their voices against social injustices, such as systemic racism, climate change, or human rights violations, can be seen as modern-day wailers. They publicly express the collective grief and frustration of oppressed or marginalized communities, urging society to acknowledge and address these issues. Their cries are often a form of lament, seeking intervention, justice, and restoration.

Mental Health Professionals

Grief counselors and therapists often take on the role of modern wailers by guiding individuals through their pain. While they may not wail themselves, they hold space for others to express their grief and provide tools for processing it. In this way, they lead the mourning process by facilitating expressions of sorrow and offering support.

Community Mourners

Individuals who step into the space of grief alongside others, such as those who attend vigils, organize memorials, or lead moments of silence after tragedies, can also be considered wailers. They embody the collective sorrow of a group, ensuring that grief is acknowledged and shared.

Social Media Voices

In the digital age, individuals who use platforms like Twitter, Instagram, or Facebook to express grief or draw attention to global tragedies can also serve as modern-day wailers. Their posts often serve to galvanize awareness, empathy, and action, creating virtual spaces for collective lament.

Mourning Leaders in Cultural Traditions

In cultures where professional mourning is still practiced, such as in parts of Africa, the Middle East, or Asia, women (and occasionally men) who lead public mourning rituals are direct descendants of the wailing women of biblical times. They embody grief through

Call for The Wailing Women

traditional songs, cries, and rituals, uniting communities in sorrow.

Modern-day wailers are those who express grief in ways that bring communities together, acknowledge pain, and seek healing and/or transformation. Whether through activism, art, leadership, or personal empathy, these individuals serve as voices for collective sorrow and catalysts for change, embodying the timeless role of the wailing women described in Jeremiah. The call for the wailing women is a call for all of us. It is a reminder that grief is not something to be avoided or suppressed but embraced as a pathway to healing and connection with God. Wailing, mourning, and lamenting prayers are powerful tools that welcomes God into our lives, transforming our sorrow into strength and our mourning into hope. Let us heed Jeremiah's call, not only to wail and mourn but to lead others in these sacred practices. As we do, we honor the wailing women of old and join in their timeless work of leading our communities in prayer and inviting God's healing presence into our broken world.

A CALL TO ACTION

The call for the wailing women is timeless. Today, who will rise to cry out for the broken, the oppressed, and the lost? Who will mourn for the sins of our communities and intercede for restoration? Just as in Jeremiah's time, the urgency remains for skilled intercessors to lead communities into weeping and wailing through prayer until healing flows like a river. Let us respond to this call with courage, embracing our role as wailing women (and men) in a world desperate for God's mercy and restoration.

Call for The Wailing Women

A PRAYER FOR YOU

Heavenly Father, we come before You with broken hearts, humbled by the weight of our sin and the pain of our communities. Like the wailing women of old, we lift our voices in lament, crying out for Your mercy and intervention.
Lord, teach us to mourn with those who mourn, to weep with those who weep, and to intercede for the brokenhearted. Let our tears move Your heart and bring healing to the broken places in our lives and our world. Strengthen us to stand and be the voices of hope and restoration in times of despair. Father, hear our cries and turn Your face toward us. Restore what has been lost, heal what has been broken, and redeem what seems beyond repair. We trust in Your promise to wipe every tear from our eyes and to bring beauty from ashes.
In Jesus' name, we pray. Amen.

BIBLIOGRAPHY

Claassens, L Juliana M. *Mourner, Mother, Midwife*, 20. Joel Rosenberg, "Jeremiah and Ezekiel," in *The Literary Guide to the Bible*, Robert Alter and Frank

Kermode, eds. (Cambridge: Belknap, 1987), 186.

_____. Calling the keeners: the image of the wailing woman as symbol of survival in a traumatized world." Journal Of Feminist Studies In Religion 26, no. 1: 63-77. ATLA Religion Database with ATLASerials, EBSCOhost (accessed June 13, 2013).

Davis, Ellen F. *Getting Involved with God: Rediscovering the Old Testament.* Lanham, MD: Cowley Publications, 2001.

Draper, Charles W., Brand, Chad, and England, Archie eds., Holman Illustrated Bible Dictionary, Revised ed. (Chattanooga: Holman Reference, 2003).

Douglas, J. D. and Tenney, Merrill C. Zondervan's Pictorial Bible Dictionary, Supersaver ed. (Maplewood, N.J.: Zondervan, 1999).

Feminist Studies In Religion 26, no. 1: 63-77. ATLA Religion Database with ATLASerials, EBSCOhost (accessed June 13, 2013).

Grace Community Fellowship, The Grace Institute, June 13, 2013, accessed June 13, 2013, http://www.gcfweb.org/institute/prophet/jeremiah-1.html.

Grant, Amy. "Better Than a Hallelujah," elyrics.net, June 13, 2013, accessed June 13, 2013, http://www.elyrics.net/read/a/amy-grant-lyrics/better-than-a-hallelujah-lyrics.html.

Knight, George W. *The Illustrated Guide to Bible Customs and Curiosities.* Uhrichsville, OH: Barbour Publication., 2007.

Lalleman, Hetty. Jeremiah and Lamentations. Tyndale Old Testament Commentaries, vol. 21. Downers Grove: InterVarsity Press, 2013, 122.

Lipton, Diana. "Early Mourning? Petitionary versus Posthumous Ritual in Ezekiel xxiv." *Vetus Testamentum* 56, no. 2 (2006): 185–202. Accessed Nov. 2, 2019, https://search.ebscohost.com/login.aspx?direct=true&db=rfh&AN=ATLA0001513137&site=ehost-live.

Lundbom, Jack R. Jeremiah 1-20 (the Anchor Yale Bible Commentaries) (Nashville: Yale University Press, 1999)

Hetty Lalleman, Jeremiah and Lamentations. (Downers Grove, IL: IVP Academic, 2013).

O'Connor, Kathleen M. Jeremiah: Pain and Promise. Minneapolis: Fortress Press, 1997.

_____. "The Tears of God and Divine Character in Jeremiah 2-9," in *God in the Fray: A Tribute to Walter Brueggemann*, Tod Linafelt and Timothy K. Beal, eds. (Minneapolis: Fortress Press, 1980, 172–185.

Online Etymology Dictionary. "Wail." Accessed December 28, 2024. https://www.etymonline.com/word/wail.

Purkis, Suzanne. "The Etymology of Death, Grief, and Mourning." Apoplectic Apostrophes Confessions of a Grammar Ghoul (December 3, 2015). Accessed July 5, 2020, https://lucidedit.wordpress.com/2015/12/03/the-etomology-of-death-grief-and-mourning/.

Rosenberg, Joel. "Jeremiah and Ezekiel," in *The Literary Guide to the Bible*, Robert Alter and Frank Kermode, eds. (Cambridge: Belknap, 1987), 186.

Sharprio, Rabbi Kalonymus Kalman. quoted in Herbert J. Levine, *Sing Unto God a New Song: A Contemporary Reading of the Psalms* (Bloomington: Indiana University Press, 1995), 219.

Strelan, Rick, "To Sit Is to Mourn: The Women at the Tomb (Matthew 27:61)," *Colloquium* 31, no. 1 (May 1999): 31–45, accessed October 12, 2019, http://search.ebscohost.com/login.aspx?direct=true&db=rfh&AN=ATLA0000987780&site=ehost-live.

Wolfelt, Allen. "Grief?" Center for Loss and Life Transition. Accessed March 8, 2019, http://www.centerforloss.com/grief/.

ABOUT THE CONTRIBUTOR

Rev. Dr. Tammy Isaac is a licensed ordained Minister and a dedicated Chaplain. With extensive credentials, she is a Certified Life

Coach, Advanced Grief Counselor, and Board-Certified Christian Counselor. Dr. Isaac has authored several impactful books and runs a private counseling practice called Breathe Counseling Center, specializing in Grief Recovery Support. Her rich background in Chaplaincy, combined with her expertise in grief, allows her to provide compassionate care and guidance to those in need. Additionally, she is the host of the Permission to Breathe podcast, available on Spotify and Apple, where she explores topics related to healing and personal growth.

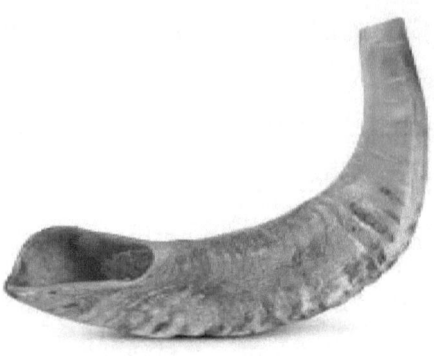

5

CALL FOR THE ELDERS

Janika Johnson-Williams

Have you ever experienced a time in your life when you were in desperate need of healing? Perhaps it was a physical ailment that left you weak and vulnerable, an emotional wound that felt impossible to mend, or a spiritual dryness that made you feel distant from God. In those moments, where did you turn? Who did you call on? The call for the elders, as

Call for The Elders

outlined in *James* 5:14-16, reminds us that God has provided a path for healing—not just individually, but through the collective faith and intercession of the church. Whether it's sickness in our bodies, brokenness in our hearts, or weariness in our souls, God invites us to lean on one another, particularly the spiritual leaders He has appointed, to seek His presence and power.

An elder is a person who is mature in their faith and has the knowledge, experience, skill set, and expertise to know God's Word and ways. Elder-led prayer is vital to helping people of the Christian faith learn how to pray when sick and for every area of their lives. Most people are unsure if they can pray properly to reach heaven. The proper prayers make a difference in one being healed versus remaining sick with the possibility of even death. Elders in the Church have been praying for centuries, years, months, days, and hours and are praying now. When one is sick, knowing that God's vessel is present and equipped with specific and compelling prayers is vital to being healed and living a healthy life. This chapter is a call to recognize the divine power of intercession, the role of elders in bringing us into God's presence for healing, and the assurance that "the effectual fervent prayer of a righteous man availeth much." Whether you've experienced healing or are still waiting for it, this promise remains true: God hears, God heals, and God restores through the faithful prayers of His people.

SCRIPTURAL FOUNDATION

James 5:14-16 instructs believers who are sick, to call upon the elders of the Church to pray for them, along with anointing them with the anointing oil in the name of the Lord. In every circumstance of life, we should go to the Lord in prayer. When we are in trouble, we should approach God honestly and humbly. In rejoicing, we should lift our hearts to God in praise. We should recognize God as the Creator of all things, including the experiences we face and the circumstances we must navigate and endure. There are times that Christians might believe that one becomes sick because of the sin that one has committed. Sometimes sickness is a direct result of sin in a person's life, other times, this is not the case. Another way sickness can enter one's body is when one chooses to be unhealthy, not wanting to follow any healthy recommendations by a healthcare provider, licensed professional, or nutrition coach. Satan is another element that has caused many people in the Bible to suffer from sickness. In the Bible, Satan is often depicted as an adversary who causes suffering, including sickness, as part of his attempts to undermine God's people. For example, in the story of Job, Satan directly afflicts Job with painful sores to test his faithfulness to God (*Job* 2:7). Similarly, Jesus frequently healed people suffering from infirmities attributed to demonic oppression, such as the woman crippled for 18 years, whom He described as "bound by Satan" (*Luke* 13:16). These examples show how Satan can be a source of physical and spiritual suffering, highlighting the need for God's power and intercession to overcome such trials. It is important to recognize that there are times when God will allow the enemy to have his way to receive the honor and glory out of the situation and circumstance.

Let's take Job for an example. Job had true faith in God and depended upon God for everything in life. Satan was granted to have his way with Job to see if he would curse God in going through the many afflictions in life along with dealing with loss. According to *Job* 17, Job was at the break of giving up on life.

Further down in scripture, Job even gave final words to his friends as a sign that he was on the verge of giving up. Job had to remain strong in his faith no matter what came to him. Scripture also tells us that Job's friends even wondered what he had done wrong in life to deserve all the noted afflictions.

Job 42:2 states, *"Then Job replied to the* LORD: *"I know that you can do all things, no purpose of yours can be thwarted."* Job represents patience and faith in adversity. When one is down, sick, or even disappointed, depending on who the individual chooses to call or reach out to, it can determine their healing process; from the scriptural foundation, the Lord will raise them and forgive their sins. Regarding Job, he had to repent unto God for not knowing who God was as the creator of all things. God healed Job and blessed him with more than he thought he had lost. God's Word never leaves us without direction. *James 5:14-*

16 tells us who to call and how the elders should pray for us utilizing the anointing oil. The ultimate intent for anyone dealing with sickness here is to be healed and free from sickness.

SPIRITUAL LEADERSHIP AND CARE

Elders within a church are mature in the faith. This level of maturity comes with the knowledge of God's Word and experience working with God's chosen people with higher expertise. Leadership in a church setting is vital to the Church's sustainability. Spiritual leaders are capable of helping someone push through in trials and tribulations by being led in study, being led in prayer, and being led in worship. The goal is to equip God's people with the tools to develop themselves and have a prosperous relationship with our heavenly Father. We as children must also develop true discernment when being led. Discernment is given to us as children of God by God as a mechanism to obtain spiritual guidance and understanding. The elders of the Church must also care about God's people. Caring about God's people is imperative to the success of their walk with Christ. We, as God's people, should also care about the elders.

Gray hair is a crown of splendor, attained in the way of righteousness. Proverbs 16:31

Eldership (Or being an Elder) is a spiritual leadership role that can be utilized at any time of the day, and it has many capable responsibilities. This spiritual leader must be able to answer the call when needed. This role is significant to God's heart because, in this role, one might be called upon at any time of the day or night. Elders must learn how to put their needs aside for the betterment of God's people when needed. Sometimes, life-or-death situations arise, and how the person is handled and directed will be vital to healing them amid a difficult situation.

Elders of the faith are channels through which God's healing power is invoked. Elders have the authority to invoke the presence of the Holy Spirit. Elders are also able to invoke the praises of God's people. God wants His people to be healed, and their sins forgiven. The objective of seeking the elders is for the Lord to pour forth the blessings He will pour out for the person stricken. The favorable intention is to see the sick or oppressed person healed and forgiven. The ill person must also want to be healed and lifted as the Word states. As the elders seek to be vessels of healing, they must also cultivate a deep, abiding relationship with God, remaining connected to Him through prayer, worship, and obedience.

INTERCESSION FOR THE SICK

James 5:14-16 instructs us that when we are sick, we must send for the elders and desire their assistance and prayers. The elders' duties are as follows: Elders are to pray over the sick. This form of prayer reflects the belief in the Christian community that individuals can approach God to seek intervention, guidance, or blessings for others. It is rooted in the idea of fellowship and mutual care among believers. Elders must understand that the sick should be anointed with the anointing oil in the Name of the Lord. Elders must be reminded that the saving of the sick is not ascribed to the anointing oil but to prayer. Prayer over the sick must proceed from true faith. When praying for someone, elders must clearly understand the need at hand. Prayers rendered must be specific and detailed.[104]

---

[104] William MacDonald, James, Believers Bible Commentary, ed. Art Farstad (Nashville TN.: Nelson Publisher, 1995), 2242-2243.

SYMBOLISM OF OIL

According to Margaret Barker, "In Christian teaching, the holy anointing oil gave life, light, and the gift of wisdom from the Holy Spirit." [105] The custom of smearing or pouring oil on a person or object in both secular and sacred contexts is to be anointed with what will distinguish the Holy Spirit from the common and the clean from the unclean. People in scripture were anointed to recognize the Lord's divine calling upon their lives; the anointing was a physical recognition of their particular role (or office), such as king, prophet, or priest. According to Ezekiel A. Ajibade, "One must understand that the anointing oil is no ritual! It is no magic wand!"[106]

---

[105] Margaret Baker, "The holy anointing oil in Armenian tradition," *International Journal for the Study of the Christian Church* 18, no. 3 (January 2019): 188, https://doi-org.lopes.idm.oclc.org/10.1080/1474225x.2018.1510239

[106] Ezekiel A. Ajibade, "Anointing the Sick with Oil: An Exegetical Study of James 5:14-15," *Ogbomoso Journal of Theology* 13, no. 2 (2008): 175, https://search-ebscohost-

Call for The Elders

"The Spirit of the Sovereign Lord is on me, because the Lord has anointed me to proclaim good news to the poor. He has sent me to bind up the brokenhearted, to proclaim freedom for the captives and release from darkness for the prisoners, to proclaim the year of the Lord's favor and the day of vengeance of our God, to comfort all who mourn, and provide for those who grieve in Zion to bestow on them a crown of beauty instead of ashes, the oil of joy instead of mourning, and a garment of praise instead of a spirit of despair. They will be called oaks of righteousness, a planting of the Lord to display his splendor." Isa. 61:1-3

Anointing was a means of investing someone with power, such as the anointment of King Solomon upon his ascent to the throne (1 Kings 1:39), perhaps to signify divine sanctification and approval. It could also signify the consecration of someone or something for a holy purpose. Jacob anointed a pillar at Bethel, calling the place a house of God (Gen. 28:18). Aaron was anointed for the

---

com.lopes.idm.oclc.org/login.aspx?direct=true&db=rfh&AN=ATLA0
001798739&site=eds-live&scope=site

priesthood (*Exod.* 29:7), and hence, the high priest is often called the 'anointed priest' (*Lev.* 4:3-15).

Anointing with oil was a common practice in New Testament times. It was a sign of joy and thanksgiving associated with feasts (*Ps.* 23:5) but was also to be observed when fasting (*Matt.* 6:17). Anointing oil was used as an emollient in healing (*Luke* 10:34); such anointing is portrayed as an outward symbol of the miraculous healing power of the divine name (*Mark* 6:13; *James* 5:14). Members of the Church at Laodicea were instructed to buy a salve and to anoint their eyes as a symbolic cure for their spiritual blindness (*Rev.* 3:18). When Mary anoints Jesus' feet to indicate her love, he interprets the act as a symbolic preparation for his burial (*John* 12:1-8). *Mark* 16:1, the women bring spices to anoint Jesus' body as a token of final respect (*Luke* 23:56). So, as one can see, the anointing oil helps us to consecrate the willingness of God's hand to move in divine favor. Divine favor cannot be bought with physical money; it is bestowed upon you when you faithfully follow God's instructions. This is known as carrying out God's ordained will for your life.

DIVINE INTERCESSION

"Is anyone among you suffering? Let him pray. Is anyone cheerful? Let him sing praise. James 5:14, Is anyone among you sick? Let him call for the elders of the Church, and let them pray over him, anointing him with oil in the name of the Lord. 15 And the prayer of faith will save the one who is sick, and the Lord will raise him. And if he has committed sins, he will be forgiven. 16 Therefore, confess your sins to one another and pray for one another that you may be healed. The prayer of a righteous person has great power as it is working."
James 5:13-20

When there is a need, and someone realizes that they cannot address the situation in their strength, the correct posture is a posture of total dependence upon God. Intercession for the sick is God's way of working through God's vessels in healing. The primary principle of intercession is to seek God's mercy and grace on others' behalf. Intercession is lifting the needs and concerns of others to God with selfless love. There are times when prayer and intercession are used interchangeably. Intercession is valuable and impacts the world for the good. When interceding on behalf of someone sick, it is rendering a prayer unto God, including a righteous and precise prayer, declaring who God is in their perspective of being ill and submitting to God's authority in the midst of being sick. After one has gone before God in prayer, one must learn how to praise God in advance for what God will do in and throughout the life of the sick person. Praising God in advance shows that you fully trust God to do what you have asked Him to do in the rendered prayer.

"Now faith is confidence in what we hope for and assurance about what we do not see."
Hebrews 11:1

THE PRAYER OF FAITH

Faith in the Bible is defined as trusting in God and believing that God will fulfill his promises. It is also described as a way to have a genuine relationship with God. Faith consists of confidence and trust. We must learn to trust God in good times and in bad times. Our faith activates God's hand to move on our behalf. In response to the prayer of faith, it's God's will if He should heal the person who is sick. It is a prayer of faith because it's based on the promises of God's Word. We should not question how much faith the Elder possesses or even how much faith the person has in seeking healing. According to the scriptural text, the elders are called upon because they can pray with complete assurance because God has promised to raise the person when all components have been met. We must also have a prayer of faith to ask God to accomplish what He has promised in his Word and believe that such a thing will come to pass. According to Daniel R. Hayden, "The prayer offered in faith" is a prayer in the full realization that it is God's will to answer the prayer in the manner desired. Yet, it is difficult to know in any given circumstance whether it is God's will for a certain person to be healed."[107]

The community of believers is considered the Body of Christ. It is essential that the body prays for each other and not cease to pray for each other. "*So, Peter was kept in prison, but the church was earnestly praying to God for him.*" (Acts 12:5). Even though the Apostle Paul was in prison and looked hopeless, the Church

---

[107] Daniel R. Hayden, "Calling the Elders to Pray," *Bibliotheca sacra 138, no. 551 (July 1981): 263, https://search-ebscohost-com.lopes.idm.oclc.org/login.aspx?direct=true&db=rfh&AN=ATLA0 000785751&site=eds-live&scope=site*

did not stop trusting and believing God for His deliverance. That should encourage you to pray no matter the problem and continue to pray with expectation. The impact of righteous prayer includes one element—the answer to the prayer request. When one prays, The Elder is petitioning the Lord for something He can only address in their situation. This act requires the person to trust the Lord's answer. "*Again, truly I tell you that if two of you on earth agree about anything they ask for, it will be done for them by my Father in heaven.* (Matthew 18:19). This scripture reminds believers to apply faith in any situation, yielding Kingdom results.

THE PROMISE OF HEALING

Here, we will explore the promise that the prayer of faith shall save the sick and the Lord shall raise them. In *James* 5:16, Christians are directed to confess their faults to one another.

Confession is necessary for our reconciliation with God when people have tempted one another to sin or have consented to the same evil actions. James states that when we sin against someone else, we should be prompted to confess this sin to the person we have wronged. We should always pray for one another. Physical healing is connected to spiritual restoration. James also links confession, prayer, and healing together. The goal here is to be raised, forgiven, and healed simultaneously. Faith must activate the manifestation of healing, allowing healing to come forth.

Faith and healing go hand in hand. One cannot experience healing without faith. Faith and healing can be very complex. Some studies suggest that people who have faith heal more quickly and thoroughly. Faith can positively impact our bodies in a good way. *According to James 5:15, "Prayer offered in faith will make a person who is sick well."* The Bible says that God sometimes heals people by His own will and that faith is not always a condition for healing. Jesus said that the quality or quantity of faith is not as important as exercising your faith. We must understand that our faith is not in the healing but in the God that heals. God commands the elders to pray for the sick in humble confidence and obedience.

As God's chosen, we must simply put our trust in God's loving presence, promises, and power. We must be bold in asking God to do what he can in our healing. The promise in the scripture is for us to be raised and forgiven. God's children are responsible for having faith to see God's hand move. Confession is a formal statement that agrees with the Word of God. When one is praying or interceding on behalf of someone else while in the area of petition for healing, the person praying must agree with the Word concerning their healing. "The

Call for The Elders

Lord sustains them on their sickbed and restores them from their bed of illness," (Psalm 41:3). Declaring specific healing scriptures over someone who needs healing will cause their faith to cultivate the healing power of God over their life.

There are times that God wants to heal those that need healing but is unable to do so due to unbelief and a lack of faith. One must understand that unbelief is not stronger than God and hinders the ultimate power of God. The kind of unbelief that limits healing only comes out through prayer and fasting. If you are lacking faith, you must reach into the depth of the heart of the one that heals and become confident that God is able to do what he says he can do.

PRACTICAL APPLICATION FOR TODAY

Elders called to pray for the sick can begin by preparing spiritually through prayer and fasting, aligning themselves with God's will and demonstrating dependence on Him. Creating a sacred atmosphere, whether in a home, hospital, or church, invites God's presence and sets the tone for meaningful intercession. Anointing the sick with oil, as instructed in *James* 5:14, serves as a powerful act of faith and a reminder of the Holy Spirit's presence and healing power. Before praying, elders should listen to the individual's specific needs, offering personalized prayer that addresses their physical, emotional, and spiritual concerns. Incorporating scripture into the prayer, such as *Isaiah* 53:5 or *Psalm* 103:3, reinforces God's promises and strengthens faith.

Encouraging confession and forgiveness is also vital, as *James* 5:16 highlights the connection between healing and spiritual restoration. Elders should pray with unwavering faith, trusting in God's ability to heal while acknowledging His sovereignty and timing. After praying, continued support is essential through follow-ups, additional visits, or sending encouraging messages. Elders can also collaborate with medical professionals to ensure the sick receive holistic care, recognizing that God works through both spiritual and physical means. Ultimately, elders should reassure the sick of God's love and presence, offering comfort and encouragement, regardless of the immediate outcome.

Call for The Elders

ENCOURAGING COMMUNITY PARTICIPATION

The local congregation plays a vital role in supporting the sick alongside the elders. While the elders are specifically called to pray and anoint with oil, the congregation is called to create an environment of love, faith, and unity. The community can participate in this transformative experience through prayer. Their role includes interceding in prayer for the sick, as *James 5:16* encourages believers to *"pray for one another, that you may be healed."* This collective prayer demonstrates the power of community and fosters a sense of belonging for the individual in need. The local congregation must create opportunities for community outreach, in which people from the area can be in a location and truly experience the love and healing power of the Lord. The congregation can provide practical support, such as meals, transportation, or companionship, showing the love of Christ in tangible ways. I would suggest that if you are a part of a church that has Community Outreach, you should join the body in helping to reach out to those who might be sick, home and/or bedbound. Your encouragement, shared testimonies of healing, and spiritual support contribute to the faith and hope of the sick person. By embodying the hands and feet of Christ, the local congregation complements the work of the elders, ensuring that the sick is cared for holistically—spiritually, emotionally, and physically. There is value in reaching out and supporting your surrounding communities.

SUMMARY OF KEY POINTS

This chapter focused on the purpose of what an elder is in the Church along with their roles and responsibilities related to healing one's sickness according to their faith. *James 5:14-16*

Call for The Elders

instructs us on how to handle sickness and who to call. This chapter also expounds on the role of the elders and how an elder should have spiritual leadership while caring for God's chosen people. Elders are known as intercessors for the sick. Elders are also recognized as a vessel for God's healing.

Faithful prayer is vital and significant to receiving true healing when one is sick. One must stand on the promises of God for one's healing. This will help the believer know that God will do what He has said in His Word.

Some steps must be followed when healing is needed. The sick person must confess their sins or wrongdoings to God in the healing process. The ill person must have a community of believers surrounding them and cheering them on in faith. When elders are called to handle those who are sick or afflicted, the power of fervent and righteous prayers will bring about God's will for their lives. When the scripture speaks about the sick being anointed with anointing oil, one must believe that the anointing oil is set apart for God's special attention. When someone is healed and forgiven, this is when heaven meets earth. Elders can implement this call by practicing steps that follows the biblical mandate in contemporary settings. Most elders in a church are a part of encouraging community participation.

MY PERSONAL EXPERIENCE

In writing this chapter, "*Call for The Elders,*" I was reminded of the many times I personally had to rely on the prayers of elders. As a woman of faith, I have faced challenges that tested my physical and spiritual strength. After having children, I was diagnosed with several medical illnesses. Determined to improve my health, I sought out the right medical professionals, but I also made a conscious decision to partner with God and the Holy Spirit in managing my conditions. While this journey has been far from easy, God's grace has given me the strength to cope with these adjustments while fulfilling my roles as a wife and mother. Though I am still waiting for complete healing in every area of my life, I remain steadfast in my faith and trust in God's timing.

Even as I wrote this chapter, I experienced an unexpected challenge—extreme pain in my right shoulder that seemed to come out of nowhere. I had not done anything to injure it, yet the pain was intense and debilitating. In that moment, I called upon the elders to pray for me. Through their prayers and the power of God, the pain gradually subsided, and my shoulder was restored to full functionality. I thank God for every healing I have experienced and for the strength He provides daily. It is important to understand that God is our keeper, our sustainer, and our healer, working in His perfect timing. All we must do is trust Him and remain faithful, knowing that His plans for us are always good.

A CALL TO ACTION

The call to action here is to encourage the Church to embrace the call for elders to pray over the sick and for the community to support one another in prayer, believing that healing will occur for all. This reinforces the message that no one in the body of Christ walks through sickness alone. This chapter challenges the church to embody the teachings of *James 5:14-16*, creating a culture where healing is sought and celebrated as a communal act of faith, obedience, and trust in God. Faith and unity in healing are very significant and needed for total healing to take place. Having faith is what moves God's hand in your situation. Unity helps those around you know that if God can heal and lift you up, He can do this for anyone sick and afflicted. One must trust God's Word while having faith to know that his will be done for your life which is to be healed and restored. Elders are urged to step boldly into their God-given role, preparing themselves spiritually and faithfully interceding for those in need of healing. They are called to pray with conviction, anoint the sick with oil, and trust in God's promises to heal and restore.

A PRAYER FOR YOU

Heavenly Father, we come before You with hearts full of gratitude for the gift of prayer and the power You have entrusted to Your people. We thank You for the elders You have called to intercede on behalf of the sick and the hurting. May they be filled with Your Spirit, equipped with unwavering faith, and anointed to carry out their sacred duty with humility and love.
Lord, we lift up those who are dealing with sickness in their bodies today and those

interceding for sick family members or loved ones. According to Your Word in James 5:14-16, we ask that the sick will call upon the elders of the church to pray for them, anointing them with oil in the name of Jesus. May the prayer of faith make them well, and may they experience Your forgiveness and restoration. Teach us as a community of believers to confess our sins, pray for one another, and trust in Your perfect timing, knowing that the prayers of the righteous availeth much. We ask that You strengthen the bonds within Your church, uniting us in prayer and support for one another. Help us to embody Your love, bringing hope and comfort to those in need. Lord, we pray for healing, blessings, forgiveness, and restoration for all who call upon You. May they be lifted and made whole in the name of Jesus, our Healer and Savior. Amen.

BIBLIOGRAPHY

Ajibade, Ezekiel. "Anointing the Sick with Oil: An Exegetical Study of James 5:14-15." Ogbomoso Journal of Theology 13, no. 2 (2008): 175. https://search-ebscohost-com.lopes.idm.oclc.org/login.aspx?direct=true&db=rfh&AN=ATLA0001798739&site=eds-live&scope=site

Baker, Margaret. "The holy anointing oil in Armenian tradition." International Journal for the Study of the Christian Church. 18, no. 3 (January 2019): 188. https://doi-org.lopes.idm.oclc.org/10.1080/1474225x.2018.1510239

Hayden, Daniel. "Calling the Elders to Pray," Bibliotheca sacra 138, no. 551 (July 1981): 263. https://searchebscohostcom.lopes.idm.oclc.org/login.aspx?direct=true&db=rfh&AN=ATLA0000785751&site=edslive&scope=site

MacDonald, William. James. Believers Bible Commentary, edited by Art Farstad. Nashville: Nelson Publisher, 1995.

ABOUT THE CONTRIBUTOR

Lady Janika Johnson-Williams (Lady J) is the First Lady of the Foundation Worship Center. She is a devoted mother, minister, mentor, speaker, and wife who has positively influenced many lives through her ministry, powerful prayers, and unwavering dedication to service. She believes she is called by God to uplift and encourage women, being led by the Holy Spirit in all aspects of her life and ministry. Her passion for empowerment is deeply rooted in her desire to see others operate in alignment with God's Spirit. Lady J has served in various leadership roles that have refined her calling and purpose, culminating in her co-laboring to build the remarkable Foundation Worship Center. A graduate of the University of Texas Medical Branch, Lady J holds a Bachelor of Science in Nursing. She furthered her education at Texas Woman's University, earning a Master's in Health Care Administration, and later received an MBA from Amberton University. With over twenty years of nursing experience and expertise, Lady J continues to make a difference both in healthcare and ministry. In her personal life, Lady J enjoys spending quality time with her husband, their three daughters, and extended family. Her favorite scripture, Psalm 23, reflects her deep faith and trust in God's guidance.

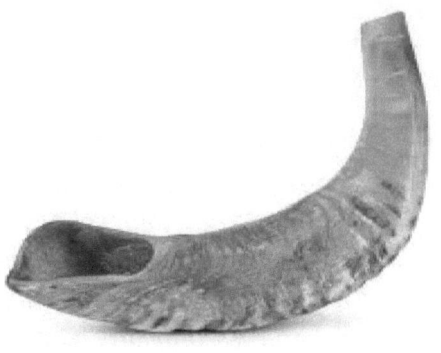

6

CALL FOR THE INTERCESSORS

(HUMANITY ANSWERING THE DIVINE CALL)

Rev. Vera Roberts

The poem "The Ministry of Intercession" by Frances Ridley Havergal beautifully captures the essence of intercessory prayer.

> THERE is no holy service
> But hath its secret bliss;
> Yet, of all blessed ministries,
> Is one so dear as this?

Call for The Intercessors

The ministry that cannot be
A wandering seraph's dower,
Enduing mortal weakness
With more than angel-power;
The ministry of purest love
Uncrossed by any fear,
That bids us meet at the Master's feet,
And keeps us very near.

God's ministers are many
For this His gracious will,
Remembrancers that day and night
This holy office fill.
While some are hushed in slumber,
Some to fresh service wake,
And thus the saintly number
No change or chance can break.
And thus the sacred courses
Are evermore fulfilled;
The tide of grace by time or place
Is never stayed or stilled...[108]

The poem "The Ministry of Intercession" reflects the profound nature of intercessory prayer, emphasizing its relational aspect and the grace it offers in God's Presence. Intercession allows us to connect warmly with

---

[108] Havergal, Frances Ridley. "Ministry of Intercession." In The Ministry of Song, 1880

Call for The Intercessors

God, the Eternal, bringing peace, love, and joy into our lives (I *Thessalonians* 5:16-18). Intercession is a divine call to humanity to intercede for our and other humans' situations. I can imagine voices of intercessors, sounding like a heavenly chorus, rising day and night with adoration, honor, and love enclosed with friendship, respect, awe, and trembling toward God, the Eternal's throne of grace and mercy.

This ministry is accessible to humanity on their journey of life on earth, enabling continual prayer. While it may seem simple, without contemplation and ineffective, true intercession involves deep communion with God, the Eternal. Furthermore, Anam Cara (Soul Friends) suffer as they journey with others and sometimes pray for hours, with no end in sight. Intercessors pray and hope for divine responses, experiencing immense joy when they receive an acknowledgment of their prayers.

This chapter addresses the concept of being "displaced," defined as those forced from their homes due to conflict or disaster. Genesis 3:23a records, *"So the Eternal God banished Adam and Eve from the garden of Eden and exiled humanity from paradise..."* Yes, God displaced humankind from our original intended habitual residence. I can imagine that our original habitual residence, Garden of Eden, was a special place; it must have provided humans with a true sense of belonging, security, comfort, and community. Also, it was where humans heard the sound of God's presence in the garden. (*Genesis 3:10*) From another perspective, we may feel displaced at times, questioning our circumstances and experiences. For example, relational, psychosocial, and emotional experiences like rejection, distress, fear, guilt,

Call for The Intercessors

bereavement, aloneness, confusion, loss, physical and emotional pain, and other challenges.

As a chaplain and Trained Spiritual Director, I often meet patients facing emergency or cosmetic surgeries. While not all patients are anxious, some are. My chaplaincy role begins with praying for awareness of the patient's urgent needs. As a Spiritual Director, I seek God's presence and guidance with each person I visit. One morning, after praying for the presence and guidance of God, as an authentic Spiritual Director, I entered the patient's room, made eye contact, smiled, introduced myself, and explained my purpose. She quickly said, "But I'm an atheist." Expecting rejection, she seemed surprised when I assured her that I cared for atheists too. Her shoulders relaxed, and she smiled slightly. With compassion, I gently asked about her support system, and she revealed she had no family or friends coming to support her. This sense of displacement moved me to pray for her. Despite feeling powerless to change her situation, intercession is my strength. We, as intercessors, rely on God, the true healer, to provide what we cannot.

Faith is crucial in intercession. Though I lacked what she needed, I have faith in God, who calls us friends. Scriptures assure us that God, the great "I AM," can surround her with supportive people. Friendship with God involves faith and closeness, as seen in *Genesis* 18:22-26, where Abraham interceded for Sodom. Trusting in a friend's character or method of operation (MO) is essential for a strong, authentic relationship. Scriptures, like *John* 15:15, highlights that God calls us friends, implying that friendship with God involves mutual understanding and trust. To be a friend, we must be friendly and genuinely seek that relationship with all our hearts.

A true friendship must have unwavering trust, even in moments of doubt, and a deep care for one another. This closeness means knowing each other well, liking each other a lot, and wanting to spend time together, as defined by the Cambridge Dictionary. In *Genesis 18:22-26*, Abraham showed his trust in God's character by pleading for the righteous in Sodom, showing his belief in God's just and merciful nature. These passages illustrate that a friend believes and trusts in their friend's MO, expecting them to act consistently with their character. Do you feel that you are a friend of God? While God calls us friends, it equally requires us to accept God as our friend. Do you willingly choose to look for and nurture this divine relationship?

Call for The Intercessors

Persistence in prayer is essential. Even when answers are delayed, we must persevere, believing in God's provision. Intercessors can face righteous doubt and expect blessings while persistently praying. Displaced humankind encompasses people, including atheists, traumatized adults/children, the homeless and refugees. With care and by faith, I confirmed my patients worth, value and genuine acceptability. Sometimes intercessors need a distinct perspective. So, I intentionally saw her through a kindhearted set of lenses; from my perspective God sees us with kindness also. With a non-judgmental presence, I actively listened with empathy, allowed time for personal reflection, and provided the ministry of presence. My prayer for the patient, with her permission, illustrated how we can choose to be a source of support for others, fostering connections through love and compassion. We believe that God is love and love is the glue of relations and relationships. Subsequently, persistence in prayer may be a demonstration of love.

Gratitude is vital. I thanked God for the opportunity to support her and pray for her acceptance and healing. Yes, the patient allowed me to pray before surgery and she expressed words of gratitude saying, "I am grateful." My faith in God, my friend, gave me hope and joy. I am convinced that God has compassion for all displaced humankind and divinely calls them into communion with Him.

Intercession connects God's love and our human frailty, inviting us to reflect on the needs/perils of humanity and the healing power of prayer. The biblical narrative of *Jeremiah 27-29 (The Voice)* reminds us that even in times of suffering and displacement, through the power of intercession, God's presence and authority prevails, offering hope and purpose.

Call for The Intercessors

THE ETERNAL, COMMANDER OF HEAVENLY ARMIES AND GOD OF ISRAEL

In Jeremiah's letter to the displaced people in Babylon, he asserted the authority of the Eternal, Commander of Heavenly Armies and God of Israel. (*Jeremiah* 27:4) He emphasized that God created the earth and had the power to give it to whomever He chooses. Jeremiah explained that God had granted Nebuchadnezzar rule over the nations, warning that any kingdom refusing to submit will face severe consequences.

Jeremiah's authority was crucial because he contended with other prophets who claimed divine inspiration. For the displaced people of Judah, this presented a dilemma: whom to believe amidst competing claims. The question remained—how do they discern true divinely inspired authority in a time of uncertainty?

DISPLACED PEOPLE IN BABYLON AND JUDAH

Displaced people, whether exiled or remaining in altered environments, faced significant challenges. They could endure protection issues, food shortages, and inadequate shelter. Exiled individuals may have experienced profound emotional trauma due to the loss of familiar surroundings and supportive networks, leading to feelings of anxiety, depression, and uncertainty about their future.

Non-exiled individuals, witnessing the disappearance of friends, businesses, and community stability, may have also experienced grief and a sense of loss. They could have felt anxious about their own safety and the stability of their families, questioning whether they might be next to face displacement. Both groups may have struggled with daily tasks, preoccupied with fears about their circumstances and the wellbeing of their loved ones.

The psychological and emotional toll of displacement—whether through direct exile or community loss—affects all humankind, fostering a shared sense of sorrow and instability.

WHAT SHOULD WE DO, NOW?

In *Jeremiah* 29:4-7, God encouraged the exiled people to grow their families and seek the peace and welfare of Babylon. They are to pray to God, so, if Babylon has peace, the exiled will live in peace. I Peter 3:8-9 record, "[8] *Finally, all of you, be like-minded and show sympathy, love, compassion, and humility to and for each* other— ⁹...It was this you were called to do, so that you might inherit a blessing."

God emphasized the importance of community and continuity. He wanted them to thrive even in captivity, which would ensure the endurance of their identity and heritage. By nurturing their families and praying for their captors, they could foster a sense of peace and resilience, which would benefit both them and the city they inhabited. This underscored God's commitment to His people and their role in a larger divine plan.

PRESENT AND FUTURE HOPE AND PROMISE IN THE PRESENCE OF GOD

God desires humanity to multiply (*Genesis* 1:28) to fulfill His command for stewardship over creation, fostering community, and expanding the expression of His image in the world. This growth reflects His abundance and the continuation of His covenant with humanity, ensuring that His purposes persist through successive generations. When we intercede[109], we participate with God in God's plan for humanity.

GOD'S PRESENCE AND PROMISES

The passage from *Jeremiah* 29:10-14 conveys God's promise to the exiled people of Judah: they would endure 70 years in Babylon but also could expect restoration and hope. God reassured them that He had plans for their peace and would certainly respond to their prayers. This promise extended beyond their immediate circumstances and emphasized God's faithfulness.

---

[109] Strongs' #6419: Palal – Greek/Hebrew Definitions – Bible Tools

Call for The Intercessors

Intercessors were encouraged by God's commitment to hear and respond to their calls. Even in displacement, they could trust in His presence and seek Him earnestly, confident that they would find Him. Biblical texts throughout the Old Testament highlight the importance of waiting on God with hope and expectancy (*Psalms* 25:21; 27:14; 40:1; 130:5), assuring believers that they will not be disappointed, (*Isaiah* 49:23).

The examples of Abraham, who interceded for Abimelech (*Genesis* 20:8-17), and the Israelites in Egypt illustrate God's active concern for the suffering and the vulnerable (Brueggermann 2001). The displacement of Judah served as a reminder of their past failures to treat their neighbors ethically (*Jeremiah* 7:5-7), highlighting the need for justice and compassion.

Job's story further emphasizes the power of intercession. God has the authority and right to rule. (*Job* 42:8) Despite his own suffering, Job prayed for his friends, demonstrating God's compassion, and leading to his restoration. (*Job* 42:10) These narratives collectively affirm God's relational nature and His unwavering promises to His people, even amid trials and displacement.

In the Acts of the Apostles, we read about the significance of prayer and intercession in God's plan of redemption. The giving of the Holy Spirit teaches us the importance of prayer on earth. Acts 1:13a records, "*This whole group [apostles/disciples of Jesus] devoted themselves to constant prayer with one accord...*" The story of Pentecost necessarily included prayer and intercession, the filling with the Holy Spirit, the bold and powerful speaking of God's word, and the demonstration of unity and love. As displaced humans, the apostles were set apart for as much to prayer as to the ministry of the word. Prayer and intercession were at the core of the spiritual life and power of the church. God as a father gave the Holy Spirit to them who asked as a child. *(Luke 11:13)* The apostles willingly and unapologetically answered the divine call to prayer and intercession.

WHO ARE THE DISPLACED PEOPLE IN OUR CENTURY?

In our century, displaced humankind encompasses a wide range of individuals affected by various crises, including armed conflict, persecution, natural disasters, and pandemics. The COVID-19 pandemic notably led to widespread isolation and displacement, impacting millions globally. On the National Day of Prayer Website, we read in 2020 that the National Day of Prayer Task Force with intercessors led the nation to embrace God-given creativity. They pivoted their normal prayer formats to use video, chat, and phone calls for praying.

Faith communities, like those at the Kingdom Builder Center in Houston, responded by creating initiatives such as the National Prayer Connection (NPC), where intercessors, displaced but united in prayer, reflects a collective resilience and support network during those challenging times.

The NPC, initiative in reaction to the pandemic, has become a sustained coalition of prayer, involving thousands across the U.S. This effort illustrates how communities can adapt and maintain spiritual connections even when physically separated. Such initiatives resonate with the call to intercede for others, aligning with scriptural teachings that emphasize love and prayer for those who face hardships. This context displays the enduring strength of faith and community amidst displacement and crisis.

HUMANITY'S TRANSITION

Humankind also faces challenges such as stress, fear, and depression, prompting a need for various forms of supportive care—spiritual, physical, financial, legal, psychological, and social. During transitions, individuals may question their purpose and hope in God's presence. However, like Abraham, who exemplified faith, believers can trust in God's MO, promises, and hold onto hope. (Hebrews 6:18)

The Ministry of Intercession emphasizes God's deep concern for humanity, aiming to foster inner joy and fulfillment. It invites individuals to accept God's unconditional love, unquestionable acceptance, and transformation through Jesus, the Christ by the activities of the Holy Spirit, suggesting that this divine calling elevates our lives and character.

The poem associated with this ministry reflects the accessibility of prayer for humankind, allowing all to bring their needs before God. With courage, intercessors wait expectantly for God's responses, praying with humbleness and genuineness.

As new intercessors reflect on their spiritual journeys, they are to appreciate their friendship with God and to be open to His acceptance. In moments of weakness, believers accept reassurance by scripture that the Holy Spirit intercedes on their behalf, articulating prayers when they are unable to do so, (*Romans* 8:25-28).

QUESTIONS FOR YOUR CONTEMPLATION

1. Since intercession starts with a personal relationship with God, how do you personally cultivate your friendship with God in your daily life?
2. Can you think of a moment when you perceived God's friendship in a profound way?
3. How do you encourage others to accept, build and maintain a close relationship with God?
4. How does trusting God's method of operation (MO) influence your prayers and intercessions?
5. If you are a current intercessor, what inspired you to answer the divine call?
6. How do you prepare yourself spiritually and emotionally before interceding for others?
7. How do you approach individuals with different spiritual beliefs or no spiritual beliefs?
8. What personal experience have you had where intercession brought peace, love, or joy into your life?
9. Is it possible to share a story with others where persistence in prayer led to a significant breakthrough? What story would you share with others?

10. What other biblical narratives can we study to strengthen our belief in and practice of intercession?

I pray for the peace of God, the Father, Jesus, the Christ, and the Holy Spirit to be with you! Amen.

A CALL TO ACTION

This chapter calls on readers to embrace the Ministry of Intercession and connect with other intercessors, emphasizing a collective pursuit of divine connection and purpose.

TODAY is the day! "CHOOSE THIS DAY and EVERY DAY" to respond to GOD's call to intercede with willing hearts and fervent prayer! The Ministry of Intercession is not just a duty—it's a sacred privilege to partner with GOD's heart, standing in the gap for others and witnessing His transformative power.

Call for The Intercessors

Through intercession, we align with God's deep concern for humanity, embracing His unconditional love and allowing the Holy Spirit to elevate our lives and character. In this ministry, we find inner joy, fulfillment, and the power to make an eternal impact.

Will you answer the call? When you sense the urge of GOD's Spirit, step boldly into prayer, knowing that your obedience draws heaven closer to earth. Choose to be a vessel through which God's love flows and watch as He works wonders through your prayers. The call is clear. The need is urgent. Will you intercede?

A PRAYER FOR YOU

Heavenly Father,
I thank You for the awareness You have given to this precious reader—the awareness of Your voice, Your calling, and Your grace. Lord, at any time or season of their life, when they feel the gentle nudge or the powerful impulse to pray, may they recognize it as an invitation

Call for The Intercessors

into deeper relationship with You. Thank You for allowing them to see the beauty and power of this divine connection.

I praise You, Lord, for their willingness to answer the sacred call of intercession. May they know deep in their spirit that their prayers matter, that they are heard, and that through them, heaven touches earth. Bless them with the confidence that they belong in this ministry, chosen by You to stand in the gap for humanity.

Lord, strengthen them as they step into this holy work. Fill them with Your Spirit, guide their words, and grant them a heart full of compassion and faith. Remind them daily that this calling is not a burden but a gift—a way to reflect Your love and bring Your will to pass.

YES, Lord! They belong to You and to this divine work. Hallelujah and Amen!
In the mighty name of Jesus, I pray, Amen.

BIBLIOGRAPHY

All Scripture quotations in this chapter are from the Holy Bible, The VOICE translation, Copyright @ 2012 by Ecclesia Bible Society

Call for The Intercessors

Baker's Evangelical Dictionary of Biblical Theology 1997. Edited by Walter A. Elwell –

Brueggermann, Walter. 2001. *Abingdon Old Testament Commentaries Deuteronomy*. Nashville, TN: Abingdon Press.

Cambridge Dictionary. 2024. "Closeness." CambridgeWords. October 23, 2024. https://dictionary.cambridge.org/dictionary/english/closeness#google_vignette.

Havergal, Frances Ridley. "Ministry of Intercession." In The Ministry of Song, 1880

Kingdom Builders: The Prayer Institute." "Taking The World by Prayer!" Last modified May 15, 2023. Accessed March 5, 2020. https://www.prayerinstitute.com/about-us/. National Day of Prayer Task Force. *National Day of Prayer*. Accessed May 5, 2020. https://www.nationaldayofprayer.org/

Strong's 6419 Strongs' #6419: Palal - Greek/Hebrew Definitions - Bible Tools

ABOUT THE CONTRIBUTOR

Rev. Vera Roberts, originally from Louisiana, relocated to Houston, Texas, where she has built a distinguished career in ministry and chaplaincy. A certified Crisis Counselor, she holds a Master of Divinity with a certificate in Pastoral Care from Southern Methodist University. Rev. Roberts has served as a licensed Senior Pastor in the Texas Annual Conference (TAC) of the United Methodist Church, a delegate to the South District of the TAC, and has been commissioned as a Trained Spiritual Director by the TAC. She completed her Clinical Pastoral Education residency at Houston Methodist Hospital and is currently a Board-Certified Chaplain with the Association of Professional Chaplains. Known for her contemplative nature and empathetic listening, Rev. Roberts brings joy and peace to every moment. In her free time, she enjoys

Call for The Intercessors

practicing Qigong, gardening, and listening to meditative music for self-care.

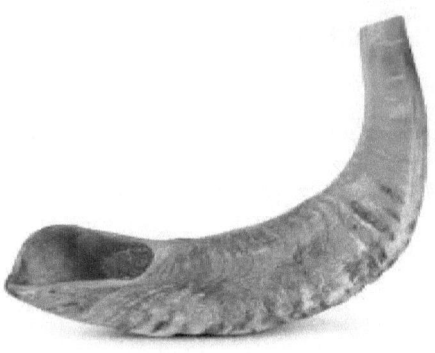

7

CALL FOR THE PRAYING MOTHER

Latrice Sumuel

One of the most profound experiences shared by women of all ages and backgrounds is the journey of nurturing and creation. Whether through motherhood, caregiving, mentorship, or acts of love and kindness, women carry within them the ability to cultivate life in many forms. This journey resonates deeply across cultures, transcending biological motherhood and celebrating the essence of womanhood as a powerful, God-given gift. It is a moment of sisterhood, a symbol of creation, and a reminder that the power to nurture, uplift, and inspire others exists within every woman.

There may be great excitement and joy going through the phases of becoming a mother. Within the journey, there are also moments of reflecting on the what ifs and the uncertainties that could arise during the stages of pregnancy as well as motherhood. In this case, many women do much research to gain wisdom and knowledge about having a successful pregnancy. After all the research and changes that are happening physically and mentally, something shifts in the time that a mother spends with her seed in the womb, which creates deep intimacy that builds unity and a connection that only a mother and a child share. As this deep intimacy develops, it lays the foundation for the dynamic relationship that will continue to evolve outside the womb.

Children look up to their parents as heroes who can save them from everything, and parents will do everything possible to protect, provide, and pour into their children, with every fiber of their being. Children often experience and engage in the physical expressions of love and care provided by their parents—the laughter, joy, and quality time that form the foundation of family life. However, they are often unaware of the countless prayers and declarations spoken over their lives, even before they were born. Mothers are essentially designed to nurture, and in this role, the act of prayer becomes a more intentional practice, recognizing that they cannot always be physically present with their children. Still, we believe that God is

Call for The Praying Mother

watching over them, when we are not in their presence.

Prayer is the driving force that creates connections through the Holy Spirit based on the intimate time we spend together. We sit in solitude and become free to release our concerns in the care of the one who we know can and will work all things out behind the scenes on our behalf. The more we stay in the secret place, the more equipped we become to stand and face challenges, despite the circumstances, because we know the extra layer of strength, courage, and covering that comes from God. Parents cultivate essential relationships with their children, with motherhood being a significant aspect of this dynamic. In motherhood, children turn to their mother in celebrations, adversity, and transitions, seeking her comfort, strength, and the power to keep moving forward. While we may have the right words, perfect hugs, and answers, we trust in the guiding hand of God to lead our children through life. This supporting relationship not only fosters resilience but also instills confidence in children, enabling them to approach life's challenges with determination, knowing they have a steadfast and unwavering supporter by their side. This dependence on God's guidance gives us, as mothers, the reassurance and confidence to face the challenges of motherhood, and it is a testament to the power of prayer in our lives.

In 1 Samuel chapters 1-2, we discover the power of prayer through Hannah. Now, let me set the picture for you: Hannah was married to Elkanah, who was also married to Peninah. Peninnah had children, and Hannah did not but she desired to have children. Hannah dealt with infertility issues, and Peninnah provoked her because she was unable to conceive children. Hannah was broken and had to witness Peninnah nurture her children in the same household. She wondered when she would experience motherhood. Instead of Hannah giving her energy to Peninnah, she went to the Lord in prayer. *"Hannah wept much and prayed to the Lord. And she made a vow, saying, "O Lord Almighty, if you will only look upon your servant's misery and remember me, and not forget your servant but give her a son, then I will give him to the Lord for all the days of his life, and no razor will ever be used on his head"*, 1 Samuel 10-12 (NIV). Hannah wept with the Lord until He answered her prayer. It was because of her faithfulness and obedience; God blessed Hannah's womb with a child whose name would be Samuel. Samuel was protected by God and covered in the will of God because of his mother's prayer. Hannah sacrificed giving Samuel over to God. In doing so her heart was pleased because her prayer was answered, and he was in the best hands ever, the hands of God.

THE IMPORTANCE OF MATERNAL PRAYER

"Love does not delight in evil but rejoices with truth. It always protects, always trust, always hopes, always perseveres"
1 Corinthians 13:6-7, (NIV).

A mother's engagement in prayer is firmly anchored in the deep love she has for her family. Prayer is the shield that protects the family from danger, both seen and unseen. This protection comes from the strong connections built through God and the mother. Once our relationship as mothers is built with God, He begins to answer our prayers, we can see His Work as the Father, working within our children. When we pray for our children, we allow God's work to be done through them and by Him. We are also creating an atmosphere where prayer becomes the foundation of their lives from childhood to adulthood so they will remember

Call for The Praying Mother

to pray and use prayer as their anchor to navigate life.

When I was 25 years old, I lost my mother to Metastatic breast cancer, and as there are no words to describe the feeling then or now, I remember feeling as if life was over. It was complex and challenging to navigate through everyday living when a piece of me was numb. During this journey of grief, I remember many people expressing to me I was strong, and over time, I realized it wasn't me physically being strong; it was a spiritual connection through God, cultivated by my mother, which kept me. The small talks with Jesus, the prayers, the moments of worship, and the solitude kept me in perfect peace while processing grief and life. In those moments I could have lost my mind, but the power of prayer saved me from myself. I would have not known how to pray or why praying was so important if I had never been exposed to prayer as a child. My grandmother taught her grandchildren Psalms 23 and had us recite it every night before bed. In addition, my mother would pray over us every night before bed and every morning before school. I remember times when I witnessed my family praying through times of adversity or in emergencies and believed that God was still in control despite the outcome. This cultivated a prayer life in me because I knew one day I would need God and one day I would not be able to call on my mother, and I needed a safe place to be loved, heard, and lifted. This is the power of a prayer life and the importance of prayer with our families because one day, the little child will have to navigate through life without their mother, and prayer will be their anchor if they know how and why to pray.

BIBLICAL FOUNDATIONS FOR A PRAYING MOTHER

In 2 Timothy, verses 1-5, Timothy was instilled with the faith of his mother, Eunice, and grandmother throughout his childhood. This shows how biblical principles, and teaching can be modeled by parents from birth and passed down from generation to generation. Mothers are the first role models that children observe; this is the impact of *"Train up a child in the way he should go, and when he is old, he will not turn from it"*, (Proverbs 22:6 (NIV). The scripture focuses more on guiding children to make wise decisions and knowing how to navigate through muddy waters with the wisdom of God. We guide them how to pray, make wise decisions, and develop a relationship with God by modeling these practices ourselves and demonstrating how to navigate the ups and downs of life.

Call for The Praying Mother

We know the enemy comes to kill, steal, and destroy, and as mothers, we intercede on behalf of our children to protect them from danger seen and unseen. Standing in the gap, we open the airways for God to tune in and hear our prayers. *"The tongue has the power of life and death, and those who love it will eat its fruit.",* Proverbs 18-21 (NIV). Words have power, and when we intercede over our children, we speak over their lives to protect them from the schemes of the enemy. While we can't be everywhere the feet of our children are, our prayers will follow them all the days of their lives, and just when they feel the pressure of the world boxing them in, God will meet them right where they are and speak to their heart and remind them of their voice, to pray through it and ensure them they are not alone.

In Luke 18: 1-8, there is a widow who keeps coming to a judge, asking him to grant her justice against her adversary. Now, this judge neither feared God nor cared about men, but this did not stop her from asking for justice or a resolve. Due to her persistence, the judge granted her justice because she constantly showed up and pleaded her case until, she received an answer. *"Then Jesus told his disciples a parable to show them that they should always pray and not give up."* (Luke 18:1, NIV). The widow faced a pressing matter affecting her life. Although she did not know the outcome, she refused to allow the judge to have the final answer. She continued to stay persistent until God made way for her, which is why, as mothers, we have a charge to pray for our children regardless of their circumstances or stance; we pray because:

1. We trust and believe in God and know that all things are possible.
2. We believe there is power in prayer, and prayer can change things.

3. We believe faith without works is dead; therefore, we must execute our faith.
4. We must make our request known to the Lord until we receive an answer.
5. We believe that God hears the prayers of His children, who are called by His name, and is confident that God is in control, despite the obstacles.

Even when our prayers go un-answered, we must continue to pray to the Lord and trust in him, as the scripture reads, *"Trust in the Lord with all your heart and lean not on your own understanding; in all your ways acknowledge him, and he will make your paths straight"* (Proverbs 3:5-6, NIV). We must trust in Him and dwell with Him daily to see His light shine upon us. Everything that we desire for God to accomplish in our children's lives, start with the relationship we develop with God through prayer.

Call for The Praying Mother

We as Mothers may not have all the answers and the knowledge to understand or reach our children, but God can supply us with wisdom and knowledge as we navigate motherhood.

> *"If any of you lacks wisdom, he should ask God who gives generously to all without finding fault, and it will be given to him"*
> James 1:5 (NIV).

Mothers, we must build a strong foundation with God and operate with the wisdom of God. When we seek God for ourselves, we allow God to order our steps, give us trustworthy guidance, and help us stay steadfast with his love and grace. If we intercede on behalf of our children, we must ask God for discernment and know what to pray and how to pray. God will give us exactly what we need when we stay in constant communication with him and apply the word of God to our lives when we operate with the

Call for The Praying Mother

Holy Spirit. How do we stay connected to the Holy Spirit so that we are equipped to cover our children?

- Set aside daily time with God and connect with the Holy Spirit
- Set aside daily time to worship and praise God.
- Set aside a time of solitude to hear from God.
- Be willing to surrender to God's will for your life and listen to His voice.
- Apply the word of God to your life and your family life.

The more we become intentional about our walk with God, the more we increase our prayer life for our family. When we take the time to spend with God, we create a safe space to express our thoughts and concerns in a secret place, waiting for the guidance of God to help us make the right decision or plan of action to take. Establishing a daily practice of communication with God, allows us to deepen our understanding of His love and guidance. In those quiet moments, we can seek wisdom and find relief in His presence. This intentional time fosters our spirit, strengthens our faith, and equips us to face life's challenges with grace and confidence, to cultivate a prayer life not just for us, but our family, children and others we encounter.

PRACTICAL GUIDANCE FOR MOTHERS IN PRAYER

We know that we need time with God and have the heart to pray for our children and be the role models they need to help them in their journey. In addition, we also know that the devil is constantly trying to occupy our minds and lives with worldly things in an attempt to cause us to lose focus on God's vision for our life. The devil knows that if we are committed to God's vision for our life and family, we will receive the blessings attached to our lineage. I pray to witness the Lord's work flowing from one generation to the next: that's the power of never seeing the righteousness forsaken, God's hands working it out, and the power of believing and surrendering to the Holy Spirit.

Hannah was praying and weeping for so long that Elijah thought she was drunk, but she was passionately seeking God until He answered her prayer, and He did. She knew her time seeking God was vital to her journey of motherhood. We serve a Big God who can do exceedingly and abundantly in our lives, and the only one irritated is the devil. This is why it is important that even with the demands on our lives as mothers, we must find time to spend with God. Some of the ways we can cultivate a lifestyle of prayer amid motherhood demands are:

- Choose a specific time to pray each day and try to commit to that time.

- Write down small prayers on sticky notes and place them on a mirror that you spend the most time in during your morning routine.
- Create a prayer journal and write down daily prayers during your lunch break.
- Pray during your lunch break for at least five minutes daily.
- Before your child leaves for school, create a small prayer that can be read together daily.
- Before bed, make time to pray together as a family, set a specific time at night to pray with the family.
- Have small talks with God throughout the day.
- Ask your child if there is anything they desire you to pray for.
- Read scriptures with your children and allow them to recite them.
- Allow your children an opportunity to pray and experience God for themselves.

At times, we may feel that our prayers need to be elaborate or imitate the prayers we've seen or heard from others. However, God simply desires for us to come to Him authentically, embracing the person He created us to be. Praying can sometimes feel challenging, especially when we're unsure what to say. A good starting point is to pray for our children's salvation, protection, wisdom, and purpose.

PRAYERS TO PRAY OVER CHILDREN

Salvation - "For God so loved the world that he gave his one and only Son, that whoever believes in him shall not perish but have eternal life" (John 3:16 NIV).

Dear God, I ask in Your name that You allow my child to believe in You and understand that You are the Son of God. May they see Your light in mine as they navigate life, illuminating their path. Allow them to confess with their mouth that You died on the cross for our sins and rose again so that we may have life. I pray they trust you and allow You to guide them through life. Speak to their heart and let them draw near to You all the days of their lives. Allow them to understand that You love them unconditionally and will guide them through all things.

Call for The Praying Mother

Protection - "So do not fear, for I am with you; do not be dismayed, for I am your God. I will strengthen you and help you; I will uphold you with my righteous right hand" (Isaiah 41:10 NIV).

> Dear God, I pray You watch over my child and place (him/her/them) under Your wings. Allow (him/her/them) to walk with strength, conquer their fears, accomplish their goals, and make wise decisions. Whenever they feel isolated or alone, wrap Your hands around them and comfort them. Touch their heart and let them feel Your presence and be surrounded by Your grace. As weapons form and adversity comes, we believe they will not prosper. Allow them to walk boldly, trusting that You are their anchor.

Wisdom - "My purpose is that they may be encouraged in heart and united in love, so that they may have full riches of complete understanding, in order that they may know the mystery of God, namely, Christ, in whom are hidden all the treasures of wisdom and knowledge" (Colossians 1:2-3, NIV).

> Dear God, guide my children through life and help them make wise decisions. Give

them wisdom and discernment to choose their friends wisely, make sound choices, and follow their hearts when facing peer pressure. Don't let them become timid or easily influenced by their peers; allow them to stand firm and believe they are enough. Help them to know that they are worthy, valuable, and loved. Keep them covered and in perfect peace through all they encounter. When they are confused, traveling the wrong road, or trying to make decisions, grant them wisdom to seek You.

Purpose - "For I know the plans I have for you, declares the Lord, plans to prosper you and not to harm you, plans to give you hope and a future" Jeremiah 29:11 (NIV).

Dear God, you created each of us in Your image and likeness. As my child discovers self, I pray they find their true purpose. Allow them to trust and lean on Your words and build a relationship with You so they may hear You. Let Your will be done in their lives and allow them to find joy in all things. Even when they can't see the light at the end of the tunnel, enlarge their capacity to press forward and believe that You are near. Touch their mind and heart so they may believe they were created with a purpose. Give them the ability to discover who they

Call for The Praying Mother

are while dealing with the pressures of life. Wrap Your hands around them and lead them to victory. We trust and believe that You will and can protect and provide for Your children, who are called by Your name.

A mother's prayer is powerful and can change lives forever. I remember when I was pregnant, I used to place headphones with gospel music over my stomach every night before bed, and I prayed this prayer over my womb. Father God, I give my daughter over to You. I pray that You cover all the days of her life and that when people encounter her, they see You. I declare that she will be blessed in all areas of her life and that favor will follow her. I pray that You protect her from dangers seen and unseen and be her ultimate provider through seasons of highs and lows. I declare that her future will be great. I know that weapons will form, but they will not prosper because the blood of Jesus shall cover her all the days of

Call for The Praying Mother

her life. Wherever her feet are planted, she shall blossom. In Jesus name, Amen.

When I tell you my daughter has been blessed beyond measure and loved by people, she has no connections to, it is truly mind-blowing. Not only has she received love, but she has also been equipped to show love to others. It is not by might, power, or luck, but by her connection with God and the power of prayer that surrounds her. As my mother taught me how to pray as a child, I am teaching my daughter how to pray, and she, at just seven years old, is teaching others the power of prayer. God is watching over us because of our obedience to honor and reverence Him.

We may not have fame or fortune, but we have favor with God that places our name in rooms no man can ever erase. This favor comes from God, who desires it for all His children. This is why, as mothers, we must remain committed to our assignment, pray for our children, love them unconditionally, and trust in God. I know it's not easy, and sometimes it may feel like nothing is changing. But Mother, keep praying!

A CALL TO ACTION

Today, I encourage you, as a mother, to stand with God and trust Him with your children. Surrender your fears, worries, and doubts to Him, knowing that He cares deeply for you and your family. Speak His promises over your children, declaring that they are loved, protected, and guided by His hand. Your dedication and devotion to praying over and for them will not only bring transformation but will also teach them how to pray and trust God for themselves. As they see your faith in action, they will learn the power of seeking God in their own lives. Have faith that God is working everything out for their good, even when you can't see it yet. It won't always be like this—your prayers matter, and God hears them. Begin now: pray boldly, trust fully, and believe that He is shaping a beautiful future for you and your children.

A PRAYER FOR YOU

Father God, in Jesus's name, I ask that You cover every mother with strength and dignity today. They face battles, seen and unseen, as they navigate the demands of their lives. Give them the courage to stand for themselves and grant them wisdom and knowledge to trust and depend on You, for You are a dependable God. We pray that You remove any doubt, fear, guilt, or shame that may be keeping them captive, and release a wind of fire so they may take a stand and move forward with You.
I ask that You give them their voice, that they may dwell in the secret place. As their cup runs dry, fill them up and send them forth with a fresh anointing and power. Let them believe they are equipped with a sound that can change generations. We ask in Your name

Call for The Praying Mother

that they find the time to dwell with You, and that You hear their prayers. Isaiah 66:13 states, "As a mother comforts her child, so I will comfort you; and you will be comforted over Jerusalem" (New International Version). Guide us with the right words to say and grant us wisdom as we parent our children, helping them make wise decisions. Show us how to discipline and love our children in ways that help them grow and evolve. Help us create a loving and safe environment where our children feel comfortable talking to us about their lives. We ask that You never leave or forsake us and that Your hands follow our children all the days of their lives, so that everything they touch shall prosper. Amen.

BIBLIOGRAPHY

The Quest Study Bible: New International Version. Grand Rapids, MI: Zondervan, 1984.

ABOUT THE CONTRIBUTOR

Latrice Sumuel holds a Bachelor of Science in Psychology with a minor in Sociology from the University of Houston and a Master of

Call for The Praying Mother

Multidisciplinary Studies in Human Services from Capella University. As an educator, she leads an all-girls group focused on promoting positivity and self-love. Latrice is deeply passionate about motivating and empowering women through inspiration and life coaching, helping them find their voice and purpose. A dedicated mother to her beautiful daughter Londyn, Latrice is also a minister and advocate for diversity and inclusiveness. Committed to giving back to her community, she believes strongly in the transformative power of affirmations and declarations to inspire personal growth and positive change.

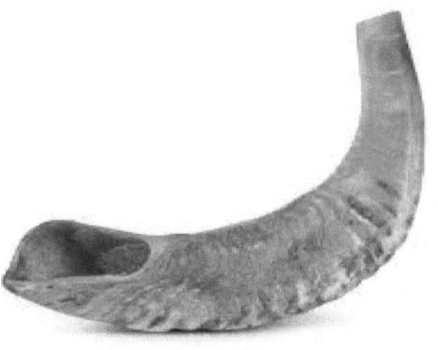

8

CALL FOR THE PROPHETIC INTERCESSOR

Dr. Henri Williams

My journey to becoming a prophetic intercessor began with my story of salvation. As a child, I was taken to church, but the values of Christianity were not genuinely lived out in our home. Much of what we practiced was more for appearances than authentic faith—meant to make others believe we were a fine, proper, and upstanding family. At the age of ten, I moved to North Carolina to live with my grandmother while my father was stationed overseas. It was there, in my grandmother's care, that I was introduced to a Pentecostal church. One Sunday, I witnessed something that left a lasting impression on me: my grandmother was "slain in the Spirit" during the service. Some friends urged me to go up and help her, but I hesitated. The entire scene both terrified and fascinated me, and it remains etched in my memory to this day.

My family often moved back and forth between North and South Carolina, staying with various relatives. My uncles didn't attend church; instead, they drank, cursed, and lived lives that seemed far removed from anything I had experienced at church. My aunts had children with different men and taught me early on to never trust a man who said, "Trust me." The only exception was my Aunt

Call for The Prophetic Intercessor

Theodore, who was married to a big, tall man who couldn't drive but was always eager to go to church. When I stayed with them, I attended their church, and going to the Southern Baptist Conferences became a regular part of my summers. I remember falling asleep during the sermons as preachers competed to see who could "hoop" the loudest or deliver the most dramatic message—slapping each other on the back and shouting fervently.

While these experiences were part of my life, they felt more like performances than genuine personal encounters with God. Growing up in a military family gave me the opportunity to travel and connect with people from all walks of life. However, it also meant that my spiritual experiences were often confined to structured, formal settings. The military's emphasis on discipline and order left little room for the spontaneous worship I had

Call for The Prophetic Intercessor

witnessed at my grandmother's Pentecostal church or the elaborate pageantry of the Southern Baptist Conventions, with their parade of hats and carefully crafted rituals.

After serving more than 30 years in various forms of ministry, I have come to realize that my true calling is to serve others through the power of prayer and intercession. Along the way, I recognized how the diverse spiritual traditions I encountered shaped me, each one contributing to my understanding of God's love and the transformative power of standing in the gap for others through prayer. What has given me the confidence to embrace what I have learned is coming to understand God's Kairos timing. Ecclesiastes 3:1-9 (NASB) reminds us that there is a time for everything under heaven. The Lord grants His intercessors an Issachar anointing—to discern times and seasons so that we may know what to do and say, especially in prophetic intercession. As 1 Chronicles 12:32 (NASB) states: "From the sons of Issachar, men who understood the times, with knowledge of what Israel should do, their chiefs were two hundred; and all their kinsmen were at their command." This anointing enables prophetic intercessors to align with God's divine timing and purposes.

It is essential to understand that many times God is ready for something to be accomplished, but He seeks someone to pray for His will to be done. When the time comes, He places His words in the mouths of intercessors, empowering them to declare His will and prepare the way for Him to perform His Word. At this point in my walk with the Lord, I have come to understand how everything my natural father demonstrated before his family profoundly impacted all five of his children—especially me—on my journey

Call for The Prophetic Intercessor

toward embracing the prophetic aspect of my intercessory calling.

Afterwards serving 30 years in the military, my father became a long-haul truck driver and eventually the Right Reverend James Henry Ruff, pastoring a non-denominational church in Fountain, Colorado. However, what I observed in him only deepened my negative feelings about hypocrisy. His actions often failed to align with the teachings of the Bible, leaving a lasting impression on me about both Christendom and the so-called men of God. I remember sitting through my father's sermons, listening to his interpretations of Scripture, yet feeling empty inside, as though something essential was missing. As I grew older and entered college, I distanced myself from the church altogether. I convinced myself that being a good person was enough, believing that God knew my heart and would forgive me for not being part of a church.

Call for The Prophetic Intercessor

During my first year of college, I stopped attending church altogether. Being away from the oppressive environment of my father's church brought a newfound sense of freedom. I made a firm decision: I wanted nothing to do with church, church people, or the so-called God they claimed to serve.

Several years later, I married a man from a Christian family. As a child, he had attended church weekly—sometimes twice on Sundays. However, once we were married, he showed no interest in church. He only went when we visited his mother's hometown. He confided in me that he had felt forced to attend church as a child, and now that he was an adult, he wasn't going to do anything he didn't want to do. With his blessing, I stayed away from church for at least three years.

As my marriage began to unravel, I found myself returning to church in search of answers. I joined a new congregation, and for the first time in years, I felt a sense of peace. I found being surrounded by godly people, worshiping, and serving in ministry made my spirit soar. I became deeply involved in several church ministries. At home, I ensured everything was in order—dinner was prepared, the house was clean, and my husband's needs were met. While my husband never stopped me from going to church, he often complained about the amount of time I spent there. At my pastor's encouragement, I invited my husband to join me, but he only attended twice in four years.

When our daughter was born, I took her to church right away. However, as a relatively new believer, I became discouraged by the behavior of some of the older women in the congregation. I overheard gossip and complaints to such an extent that I began to feel disheartened. If these women, who claimed to be "women of God," couldn't handle their issues in a godly manner, how could I expect help from them? Disillusioned, I left the church again—for three years. During that time, I separated from and later divorced my husband. I attempted to attend another church, but I left after the Associate Pastor made an inappropriate advance toward me. Feeling betrayed and broken, I stayed away from church for over a year.

My daughter and I eventually found another church to attend. However, the pastor there seemed more concerned with his image—what he wore, how his wife looked, and the type of car he drove—than teaching the Word of God. I stayed for about two years, mainly because my daughter enjoyed the children's church program. But spiritually, I wasn't being fed. I learned nothing, and my spirit remained empty. Once again, I left the church, this time for another two years. Eventually, after a long-term relationship ended, I found myself with nowhere else to turn. This time, God led me to a Methodist church, and for the first time in years, I felt spiritually nourished. The teaching was grounded in Scripture, and my understanding of God's Word deepened. My daughter had opportunities to get involved in ministry, and I began to grow in discipline, prayer, and my daily walk with God. I learned how to pray and began to experience the transformative power of Christ in my life. I witnessed God's hand move, not only in my life but also in the lives of those around me. Over time, I was healed from the negative and destructive perceptions I once held about "church people." More importantly, I developed a true, personal relationship with the Lord.

Through that Methodist church, I attended a women's conference in Detroit, Michigan, where the theme was "*How You Know You Are*

Call for The Prophetic Intercessor

Called..." After six powerful classes, I fell to my knees, weeping before God, finally acknowledging that I could hear Him speaking. In that moment of surrender, I told Him I would obey. I'll never forget the mix of reluctance and nervousness I felt as I picked up the phone to call my daughter and share the news that I had a calling on my life. Her response left me speechless: *"Only you didn't know! We've been waiting for you to accept that God is trying to use you..."* I had no idea then how the Lord would teach me to stand firmly on His Word and become a purveyor of His promises. From that moment on, Holy Spirit began to work within me in ways I now clearly recognize as preparation for ministry. It was the beginning of a transformative journey; one I will always cherish and never forget.

Holy Spirit began training my ear to hear clearly the voice of the Lord, providing instructions that, when followed, led to remarkable outcomes. Through this process, I learned that when Holy Spirit speaks, what is revealed becomes manna—either to be shared with others or to be internalized and meditated upon. I also discovered that not every revelation is meant for public consumption. Sometimes, the Word released is first intended to refine and grow the intercessor before being shared. I came to understand that I am responsible for how and when I release what God reveals to me. The way others respond to the release of His Word is not my responsibility—that is between them and God. As 1 Thessalonians 2:13 (NASB) states: *"For this reason we also constantly thank God that when you received the word of God which you heard from us, you accepted it not as the word of mere men, but as what it really is, the word of God, which also is at work in you who believe."* To that end, I understand that I will be judged by how I conduct myself in this calling. As 1 Corinthians 3:11-13 (NASB) explains: *"For*

Call for The Prophetic Intercessor

no one can lay a foundation other than the one which is laid, which is Jesus Christ. Now if anyone builds on the foundation with gold, silver, precious stones, wood, hay, or straw, each one's work will become evident; for the day will show it because it is to be revealed with fire, and the fire itself will test the quality of each one's work." Holy Spirit also taught me the power of speaking God's Word, and I witnessed the signs and wonders that followed. This partnership with Holy Spirit has transformed my prayer life. I now claim Him as my prayer partner, fully relying on His guidance to stay on task.

Accepting my calling to preach and teach the gospel has brought me peace. The mandate is clear: to set the captives free. Wherever God leads, I have learned to trust Him completely. I've asked the Lord to have His way in my life, and I am fully committed to ministering wherever and whenever He directs. In response to that calling, I began taking intentional steps toward becoming a submitted intercessor by building an authentic relationship with God, rooted in consistent time spent with Holy Spirit. I created a dedicated space in my prayer room and committed to meeting Holy Spirit there regularly. This sacred time has deepened my relationship with God and strengthened my ability to walk boldly in my calling.

I would begin my mornings by reading a daily devotional, followed by a scripture passage. Afterwards, I talked with God about what I had just read, allowing His Word to speak to my heart and guide my prayers. I would ask Him how I could best represent Him using that Scripture in the places He planned send me throughout the day. I also prayed for Holy Spirit to guide and direct me, asking that my thoughts align with His will and that my responses to others reflect the Spirit's presence within me. Most importantly, I would ask Holy Spirit to increase my love for God's people. I would create an atmosphere in my home where Holy Spirit felt welcomed. I often entered worship with music that lifted my spirit and caused me to rejoice. Even without music, I've learned that the atmosphere can be set simply by inviting His presence. Some mornings, Holy Spirit would wake me at unscheduled times, resting upon me in a way that was tangible and undeniable. As He moved across my face, a smile naturally formed on my lips, drawing me into the weight of His glory. In those moments, I felt an indescribable peace—an almost euphoric warmth that filled the room and my heart with profound joy. Many times, His presence came with a tingling sensation or a powerful sense of awe and reverence. In those sacred moments, I was reminded there was no greater joy than sensing His nearness. Whether it was the smile on my face or the deep delight in my spirit, I rejoiced in knowing He was with me. The thought of His presence made me want to lift my hands in jubilant praise, celebrating the gift of His touch and the assurance of His love. In His presence, I prayed—and still pray to this day—freely and openly to Holy Spirit in an atmosphere of praise. The God who is omnipotent, omniscient, and omnipresent knows everything about me, and it is exhilarating to know that He chooses to spend time with me. I am in awe that Holy Spirit knows the number of hairs on my head and has made me sensitive to His promptings. My deepest desire has always been to hear His voice clearly and to have a heart free from impurities.

A COMMON MISCONCEPTION

There is a common misconception that prophetic intercessors try to manipulate God to fulfill selfish desires. However, the disciplines and habits I have established in my life hold me accountable to a higher standard. I am eternally grateful for the godly men and women God has surrounded me with—people who serve as examples of faith and holiness. Their influence has been invaluable in helping me stay grounded in the truth of God's Word and the purpose He has called me to fulfill. I recommend that you, too, allow God to surround you with godly men and women in your life to hold you accountable as one who is called to the prophetic ministry. It is vital to do so, ensuring that you do not inadvertently become the very misconception that many associate with this calling.

I approach God with a willing heart, ready to lay aside everything—especially my own desires—and ask Him to reveal anything in my life that might hinder His plan for those I am meant to reach with a word of encouragement. I am reminded of Psalm 62:5 (NLT): *"Let all that I am wait quietly before God, for my hope is in Him."* When I come before a holy God, I bring every part of myself—my hidden struggles, my weariness, my frustrations, and my victories in Him—into His presence.

POSTURING YOURSELF TO HEAR

I believe that developing an intimate, relevant, and relatable relationship with the Father is key to positioning yourself to hear from Him. I strive to present my heart and my willingness to pray for others about the burdens the Lord places on my heart. When I pray, I intentionally make no negative confessions about any situation or circumstance. I stand on Psalm 17:3 (NKJV), which declares: *"You have tested my heart; You have visited me in the night; You have tried me and have found nothing; I have purposed that*

Call for The Prophetic Intercessor

my mouth shall not transgress." The Lord's requirement for a prophetic intercessor is that we purpose our mouths not to transgress by making negative confessions over anyone's situation, behavior, health challenge, loss, or gain.

Because God says we can do all things, I choose to believe His Word and come into agreement with it. When we pray, we are declaring God's promises through His Word, by faith, over every person we intercede for. I approach prayer with *tiptoe anticipation*, fully expecting that God is going to move. I believe He reveals His plans to His prophets in advance, aligning us with His will to bring His purposes to pass.

Prophetic intercession involves understanding that God desires to speak to us. Amos 3:7 (NLT) reminds us: "Indeed, the Sovereign Lord never does anything until he *reveals his plans to his servants the prophets."* This highlights the reality that the God who created all things through His spoken Word has granted humanity the privilege to do the same by aligning our words and actions with His will. I define prophetic intercession as *"hearing from God and standing in the gap for others by interceding through prayer."* It is a divine partnership where God reveals His heart, and we respond by aligning ourselves with His purpose through our prayers and declarations.

As a catalyst for moving into alignment with God's will for your life, you will come to realize that the right direction will always lead you back to His Word and His pattern for success. God uses His servants to declare what must come next. Revelation 22:6 (NLT) says: *"Then the angel said to me, 'Everything you have heard and seen is trustworthy and true. The Lord God, who inspires his prophets, has sent* his angel to tell his servants what will happen soon.'" Revelation 4:1 (NASB) continues: "After these things I looked, and behold, a door standing open in heaven, and the first voice which I had heard, like the sound of a trumpet speaking with me, said, 'Come up here, and I will show you what must take place after these things.'"

The question is are you effective in praying to the God that sees past your postering, to the genuineness in your heart that will require you to evolve in your relationship with the Father who will circumcise your heart and help you position yourself to hear from Him. Deuteronomy 30:6 (AMP) says, "And the Lord your God will circumcise your heart and the hearts of your descendants [that is, He will remove the desire to sin from your heart], so that you will love the Lord your God with all your heart and all your soul, so that you may live [as a recipient of His blessing]."

Call for The Prophetic Intercessor

HEARING GOD'S VOICE AND PRAYING IN ALIGNMENT

Hearing God's voice and praying in alignment with His will is one of the most crucial aspects of prophetic intercession. This practice involves discerning God's will and responding to His prompting, helping an intercessor cultivate a closer relationship with the Father. As prophetic intercessors grow in sensitivity to the Holy Spirit, they begin to recognize His guidance through a "still small voice," a deep sense of peace, or an impression on their heart (1 *Kings* 19:12). Regular reading and meditation on Scripture are essential because God's voice is always consistent with His Word. Time spent in prayer and worship further quiets distractions and fosters focus on the Father, making it easier to hear His voice. Often, the revelations we receive are confirmed through Scripture, circumstances, or godly counsel.

Call for The Prophetic Intercessor

A prophetic intercessor's role is to pray for God's purposes to be fulfilled and to boldly declare His promises over situations with faith and confidence (*Matthew* 6:10; *Isaiah* 55:11). This involves standing in the gap to intercede and reveal God's plans for individuals, communities, or even nations. Such alignment with God requires trust and a willingness to surrender outcomes to His perfect timing and ways. By hearing God's voice and praying in alignment with His will, a prophetic intercessor builds a unique partnership with the Father, transforming prayer into a powerful tool to bring His divine purposes to fruition on earth.

About 20 years ago, I experienced an anointing through the Holy Spirit for prophetic prayer. At the time, I didn't fully understand how to navigate many of the encounters I was having with God. I witnessed miracles and breakthroughs in response to prayer, but I also made mistakes and endured significant "growing pains" as I developed as a prophetic intercessor. Since then, by God's grace, I have served as a prayer leader, a minister on a prophetic team, and am now stepping into new roles as a prophetic writer and teacher. Each step has been part of a refining process, teaching me to trust the Father more deeply and align my prayers with His heart.

INTERCESSION

> "I urge, then, first of all, that petitions, prayers, intercession, and thanksgiving be made for all people—for kings and all those in authority, that we may live peaceful and quiet lives in all godliness and holiness. This is good, and pleases God our Savior, who wants all people to be saved and to come to a knowledge of the truth. For there is one God and one mediator between God and mankind, the man Christ Jesus, who gave himself as a ransom for all people." 1 Timothy 2:1-6 (NLT)

Call for The Prophetic Intercessor

God has called us not only to pray for our personal needs but also to intercede on behalf of others. The Greek word *Huperentugchano* translates to "intercede for" or "to fall in on behalf of someone else," signifying the act of pleading or advocating for another person. This term is often used to describe Holy Spirit's role in prayer when words fail an individual. The prefix *Huper* means "above" or "on behalf of," and *entugchano* means "to fall in with" or "to intercede."

Another Greek word, *Enteuxus*, also translates to "intercession," meaning "a meeting with" or "a petition on behalf of others." Intercessory prayer, therefore, becomes the act of seeking God's presence and making requests or petitions on someone else's behalf. When we pray for the needs of others, we engage in intercession, presenting petitions before God. As Philippians 4:6-7 (NIV) instructs: *"Do not be anxious about anything, but in every situation,*

Call for The Prophetic Intercessor

by prayer and petition, with thanksgiving, present your requests to God. And the peace of God, which transcends all understanding, will guard your hearts and your minds in Christ Jesus."

Jesus is described as the ultimate intercessor in Isaiah 53:12 (NIV): *"Therefore I will give him a portion among the great, and he will divide the spoils with the strong, because he poured out his life unto death, and was numbered with the transgressors. For he bore the sin of many and made intercession for the transgressors."* Jesus not only interceded for humanity during His time on earth but continues to intercede for us as our High Priest. As Hebrews 7:25 (NIV) reminds us: *"Therefore he is able to save completely those who come to God through him, because he always lives to intercede for them."*

Call for The Prophetic Intercessor

PROPHETIC INTERCESSION

Listen to my cry for help, my King and my God, for I pray to no one but you. Listen to my voice in the morning, Lord. Each morning, I bring my requests to you and wait expectantly.
Psalm 5:2-3, (NLT)

The Hebrew term for "prophetic" is Nabi, which means "to call" or "to proclaim." A Nabi is someone called by God to speak His words as a messenger or spokesperson. In the Old Testament, prophets like Isaiah, Jeremiah, and Ezekiel were referred to as Nabi, emphasizing their role as God's mouthpieces to communicate His will, warnings, and promises. This term highlights the active communication between God and the prophet, where the prophet serves as a vessel for divine revelation. For prophetic intercessors, the role of a Nabi involves being called to hear God's voice and intercede by bringing those revelations to God in prayer and declaring His plans. For example, in

Call for The Prophetic Intercessor

Jeremiah 1:5 (NIV), God says, "Before I formed you in the womb I knew you, before you were born, I set you apart; I appointed you as a prophet (Nabi) to the nations." This verse underscores the divine origin and purpose of the Nabi's role in God's plans.

The Greek term for "prophetic" is Prophetes, derived from pro (before or in front of) and phemi (to speak), meaning "one who speaks forth" or "a foreteller." In the New Testament, Prophet describes individuals like John the Baptist, who declared God's plans and truths. This term includes both foretelling future events and forth-telling God's Word in the present. It emphasizes the act of boldly declaring divine revelations or truths under the inspiration of Holy Spirit. For prophetic intercessors, the role of a Prophet involves speaking forth the will of God revealed in prayer, which may include both declarations of God's promises and petitions for His

Call for The Prophetic Intercessor

intervention. Acts 2:17 (NIV) illustrates this role, stating, "In the last days, God says, I will pour out my Spirit on all people. Your sons and daughters will prophesy (propheteuo), your young men will see visions, your old men will dream dreams." This verse highlights the universal nature of the prophetic calling in the New Testament era.

Both Nabi and Prophet emphasize the prophet's role as a communicator of God's will, involving divine inspiration, hearing from God, and declaring His Word. While Nabi in Hebrew culture focuses on the prophet's calling and relationship with God, Prophet in Greek culture highlights the act of proclaiming or speaking forth the message, often publicly. For prophetic intercessors, these roles intersect, as they are both called by God (like a Nabi) and equipped to declare His will and promises (like a Prophet). Prophetic intercession involves this dual role, where the intercessor listens to God in intimate communication and boldly declares His truth to align with His purposes. It is not merely about foretelling the future but about partnering with God—hearing His voice, receiving His truth, and proclaiming it in faith and obedience. This dynamic is central to prophetic intercession, as the intercessor stands in the gap, praying and declaring in alignment with God's revealed will.

A prophetic intercessor is someone called to stand in the gap on behalf of others, guided by the voice of God and empowered by His Spirit. This role goes beyond simply offering prayers; it requires stepping into the flow of God's plans, hearing His voice clearly, and aligning one's life with His purposes as revealed through His Word and Spirit. Prophetic intercession involves both advocacy and obedience, as the intercessor serves as a vessel through which God's will is declared and enacted on earth.

Call for The Prophetic Intercessor

As a prophetic intercessor, I have come to understand that God requires both obedience and submission. He places burdens on my heart to pray for others—burdens that press into my spirit with urgency until I bring those concerns before His altar. These burdens are not random but are aligned with God's will, and it is through faithful prayer and discernment that I come to understand His purpose for them. A prophetic intercessor must demonstrate a strict dependence on God, seeking His truth as the ultimate solution to every issue and concern.

Prophetic intercession is rooted in deep communication with God. The successful pattern the Lord has given me is to consistently read His Word, as it establishes the foundation for this communication. This ongoing relationship naturally leads to prophetic intercession, where God reveals His heart and plans. Through this process, I've

Call for The Prophetic Intercessor

come to realize that God not only wants to speak to us but also desires to use us as integral parts of His divine plans. This pattern is evident in Scripture. In the Old Testament, the prophet Samuel relayed God's Word to Saul in 1 Samuel 9:26-27 (MSG): *"They woke at the break of day. Samuel called to Saul on the roof, 'Get up and I'll send you off.' Saul got up and the two of them went out into the street. As they approached the outskirts of town, Samuel said to Saul, 'Tell your servant to go on ahead of us. You stay with me for a bit. I have a word of God to give you.'"* This interaction illustrates the role of prophetic intercession: to hear and relay God's Word with clarity and obedience, guiding others into His plans and purposes.

The calling of a prophetic intercessor is not new; God has always sought individuals willing to "stand in the gap" for others. Ezekiel 22:30-31 (KJV) declares: "And I sought for a man among them that should make up the

Call for The Prophetic Intercessor

hedge and stand in the gap before me for the land, that I should not destroy it: but I found none. Therefore, have I poured out mine indignation upon them; I have consumed them with the fire of my wrath: their own way have I recompensed upon their heads, saith the Lord God." This verse reveals God's heart for intercessors—those willing to step into the spiritual breach to intercede on behalf of individuals, communities, or even nations.

Prophetic intercession also demands faithfulness in action. It is not merely about hearing God's voice but responding to it in obedience and humility. The intercessor acts as a bridge between heaven and earth, declaring God's promises and seeking His intervention in the lives of others. As a prophetic intercessor, I have learned to bring every word I hear to God, asking Him to refine my understanding and guide my prayers.

Ultimately, prophetic intercession is a partnership with God. It requires sensitivity to His Spirit, a heart rooted in Scripture, and a willingness to trust His leading even when the path is unclear. This calling is both a privilege and a responsibility, as it aligns us with God's eternal purposes and allows us to participate in His redemptive work on earth.

THE CALLING AND CHARACTERISTICS OF A PROPHETIC INTERCESSOR

The prophetic intercessor is uniquely graced and anointed to pray. Prophetic intercessory prayer can be seen as an expression of the prophetic gift, flowing from the heart of a creative God who designed each of His children with unique callings. Just as no two snowflakes or fingerprints are alike, the prophetic intercessor reflects God's creativity and divine purpose. Those who walk in this

Call for The Prophetic Intercessor

calling often recognize one another as part of the same "tribe"—a family bound by shared faith, boldness, and sensitivity to the Holy Spirit. Prophetic intercessors share common characteristics that set them apart. Faith and boldness are key traits, as these intercessors must declare what God reveals, even in challenging or uncertain situations. They also demonstrate obedience, acting on the prophetic word with courage and trust, whether it involves prayer or other steps of faith. Additionally, prophetic intercessors receive revelation—insights from God through visions, dreams, impressions, or the still small voice.

One way God speaks is through impressions, which can be described as an inner voice or a "God-planted thought." These thoughts are often sudden, clear, and life-giving. For example, you may have a Bible verse drop into your mind, or a word of encouragement come to you for a friend. These are subtle yet profound ways God communicates, and many have experienced them without recognizing their divine origin. God's still small voice is not a booming, audible sound but rather a quiet, internal prompting. It may feel like a passing thought, a gentle impression, or an inner sense of His will. This is beautifully illustrated in 1 Kings 19:11-13 (NLT), where Elijah encounters God:

> Go out and stand before me on the mountain," the Lord told him. And as Elijah stood there, the Lord passed by, and a mighty windstorm hit the mountain. It was such a terrible blast that the rocks were torn loose, but the Lord was not in the wind. After the wind there was an earthquake, but the Lord was not in the earthquake. And after the earthquake there was a fire, but the Lord was not in the fire. And after the fire there was the sound of a gentle whisper. When Elijah heard it, he wrapped his face in his cloak and went out and stood at the entrance of the cave. And a voice said, "What are you doing here, Elijah?

Call for The Prophetic Intercessor

In the prophetic realm, distinctions exist between a prophetic intercessor and a prophet-intercessor. A prophetic intercessor operates within the prophetic gifting, often receiving specific insights for prayer. In contrast, a prophet-intercessor is someone who holds the five-fold ministry office of a prophet (*Ephesians* 4:11-13) and has a primary calling for intercessory prayer. These individuals often carry greater authority and are positioned to make prophetic declarations over nations, governments, or other significant arenas, including education, business, and church movements.

For prophetic intercessors, standing still and making room for God to speak is part of their spiritual inheritance. This involves creating space for God to reveal what He desires to release into the earth. As you grow in your prophetic relationship with God, you won't be satisfied with one-sided prayers. You will come to expect daily conversations with Him, knowing He always has something to say.

It's essential to remember that God speaks with purpose—to build a loving relationship with His children. His goal is never to create distance but to draw us closer. While He may convict us, it is always with the intention of restoration. Similarly, when God speaks through you to others, it is with the same heart of reconciliation and love.

Prophetic intercessors must also discern the source of what they hear. Four voices may influence you: your spirit, the Holy Spirit, evil spirits, or angels. Romans 12:2 (NASB) provides guidance: *"And do not be conformed to this world, but be transformed by the renewing of your mind, so that you may prove what the will of God is, that which is good and acceptable and perfect."* Always measure what you hear against the standard of Scripture, for God's

Word never contradicts itself. In the journey of prophetic intercession, sensitivity to the Holy Spirit, obedience, and a commitment to God's Word are crucial. As you develop in this calling, you become a vessel through which His plans are revealed, and His purposes are accomplished on earth.

PROPHETIC UNCTION

> "For prophecy never had its origin in the human will, but prophets, though human, spoke from God as they were carried along by Holy Spirit." 2 Peter 1:21 (NIV)

Prophetic unction refers to the anointing or divine empowerment given by Holy Spirit to a prophet or prophetic individual, enabling them to speak or act under God's direction. It is a spiritual enablement that allows a person to deliver God's message with clarity, authority, and accuracy, often revealing His heart, plans, or purposes. The prophetic unction originates from God and not from the individual, ensuring that the message aligns with His will and truth. As stated in 2 Peter 1:21 (NIV): *"For prophecy never had its origin in the human will, but prophets, though human, spoke from God as they were carried along by Holy Spirit."* This divine inspiration ensures that what is spoken carries the weight of God's authority.

Prophetic unction equips a person to speak with boldness and confidence, even in challenging situations. It is often accompanied by a sense of compulsion, as described by Jeremiah in Jeremiah 20:9 (NIV): *"But if I say, 'I will not mention his word or speak anymore in his name,' his word is in my heart like a fire, a fire shut up in my bones. I am weary of holding it in; indeed, I cannot."* This unction often involves heightened spiritual clarity, where the individual receives divine insight into situations, future events, or God's desires. As Amos 3:7 (NIV) reminds us: "*Surely the Sovereign Lord does nothing without revealing his plan to his servants the prophets.*" Such clarity ensures the message is rooted in God's truth, whether it is foretelling future events or forth telling His Word into present circumstances.

Operating under prophetic unction requires sensitivity to Holy Spirit, cultivated through prayer, worship, and study of Scripture. This sensitivity allows the individual to discern God's voice from personal thoughts or external influences. For example, Samuel demonstrated this sensitivity when he responded in 1 Samuel 3:10 (NIV): "*Speak, for your servant is listening.*" Additionally, prophetic unction demands obedience and submission to God's authority, as those called to this role must deliver His messages faithfully, regardless of personal feelings or how the message is received. This responsibility is emphasized in Ezekiel 2:7 (NIV): "*You must speak my words to them, whether they listen or fail to listen, for they are rebellious.*"

The purpose of prophetic unction is to reveal God's heart, whether through compassion, warnings, promises, or direction. It serves to edify and encourage the Body of Christ, bringing comfort, guidance, and alignment with God's will. As 1 Corinthians 14:3 (NIV) states: "*But the one who prophesies speaks to people for their strengthening, encouraging, and comfort.*" Prophetic unction calls individuals and communities to repentance, obedience, and greater faith, aligning them with God's divine plans. For those operating under prophetic unction, it is vital to stay rooted in prayer, maintain humility, and consistently seek God's presence to ensure faithfulness to His calling.

MY PERSONAL EXPERIENCES OF PROPHETIC UNCTION'S

I asked God to give me a few examples of prophetic unction's in my life that will bear witness with someone reading this chapter. It is my prayer Holy Spirit will quicken your spirit and bring back to your remembrance examples in your own life.

SETTEGAST APPOINTMENT – APRIL 2002

I had a client scheduled for a 10 o'clock appointment one morning, but she arrived late. As soon as she rushed in, she began apologizing profusely for her tardiness. I reassured her, saying, "No problem. I still have 45 minutes before my next client—why don't we go ahead and pray, and then we can begin our meeting?" She agreed, and we held hands as I began to pray. While praying, I felt an impression in my spirit that this woman was dealing with high blood pressure and sickle cell. I immediately began to bind those conditions, declaring that they had no authority over her body and commanding them to leave. I spoke God's promises over her, declaring that healing is the children's bread (Matthew 6), and reminding her that by the stripes on Jesus's back, she was already healed. When I finished praying, she began to cry and shared that she had been late because her earlier doctor's appointment had run over. During that appointment, she had received test results confirming she had both high blood pressure and sickle cell. In that moment, I knew Holy Spirit had allowed me to bring comfort to this woman through His Word, reminding her of God's healing promises and offering her peace in the midst of her situation.

WOMEN'S RETREAT – AUGUST 2010

I was invited to speak at a women's retreat, and as I prepared, Holy Spirit impressed upon me to bring communion cups. I agreed with what I had heard and placed my car keys on the altar where I keep my communion cups as a reminder to take them with me. However, in the rush of packing and preparing, I rushed out the door and down the road without the communion cups.

As I drove, I turned on worship music to create an atmosphere of consecration and took a deep breath, thanking God in advance for traveling mercies. While praying, I heard Holy Spirit say, "You forgot the communion cups." Although I didn't know exactly how or when the Lord planned to use them, I knew they were important, and I needed to be ready for His prompting. I spent the drive searching for a place to pick up communion cups, but none were available.

When I arrived at the retreat site, I checked in and noted that this was the church's first conference. The speaker accommodations were in a dormitory with about 20 other women. I chose the bed closest to the restroom and observed as women arrived, suitcases in hand, filled with joy and excitement. Their fellowship was warm and festive, as they shared how much they had missed each other. Sitting on my bed, I quietly listened to Holy Spirit as He began giving me impressions about the women I observed.

That evening, while the others went to the dining hall for dinner, the Lord instructed me to fast and stay behind. I spent time in His Word and prepared for the next day. Around 2:00 a.m., I found myself in the last stall of the bathroom, seeking privacy to review my notes and pray. As usual, the Lord had me weeping before Him as I processed the message I was to deliver.

My solitude was interrupted by a concerned motherly figure who knocked on the bathroom door to check on me. Despite my reassurances, she fetched some of the retreat leaders, and their genuine concern cut my time with the Lord short. I decided to get dressed and move to the conference room set aside for my session, where I could bask in the Father's presence uninterrupted.

The next morning, I fasted from breakfast and sat in the room, waiting for further insight on how to minister to the women. With worship music playing softly, I sought the Lord's direction. A young woman entered the room, carrying a bag, and said, "Pastor Henri, I brought these communion cups, and I don't even know why I brought them. Can you use them?" Tears streamed down my face as I realized the Lord's will was manifesting. I embraced her, thanked her, and continued to listen for Holy Spirit's guidance.

Holy Spirit said, "Now watch what they do when they come in. Watch what they bring into my presence and listen to their conversation. They have no understanding of reverential fear of my presence. Show them how to come before a holy God and bask in my presence, Daughter."

This moment reminded me of Exodus 33:8-11 (NLT), which teaches us how Moses reverenced the Lord and spoke with Him face to face in the Tent of Meeting, a place set apart and consecrated to God. The Scripture reads: "*Whenever Moses went out to the Tent of Meeting, all the people would get up and stand in the entrances of their own tents. They would all watch Moses until he disappeared inside. As he went into the tent, the pillar of cloud would come down and hover at its entrance while the Lord spoke with Moses. When the people saw the cloud standing at the entrance of the tent, they would stand and bow down in front of their own tents. Inside the Tent of Meeting, the Lord would speak to Moses face to face, as one speaks to a friend. Afterward Moses would return to the camp, but the young man who assisted him, Joshua son of Nun, would remain behind in the Tent of Meeting."*

This passage reveals another essential aspect of being a prophetic intercessor: having a reverential fear of the Lord. As prophetic intercessors, we must approach God with awe and respect, setting ourselves apart to hear His voice and follow His leading with humility and obedience. It is in this posture that we can fully align with His purposes and be effective vessels for His plans.

FREEDOM IN PRISON – SEPTEMBER 2019

I am part of an outreach group called Legacy Sisters, led by one of my spiritual mothers. She hosted a retreat in a cabin nestled in the

Call for The Prophetic Intercessor

woods by a beautiful lake. During this retreat, I met some amazing women who became my sisters in Christ. My natural sister, Gloria, flew in from Colorado to join us, and the Lord allowed her to relax in the safety of good company. Over the weekend, we broke bread, laughed, shared testimonies, and sought the Lord together. It was a sacred time for a core group of believers to set ourselves apart for Him.

That weekend, God performed spiritual surgery without violating the flesh. We left the retreat with new hearts, just as promised in Ezekiel 36:26-27 (NKJV): *"I will give you a new heart and put a new spirit within you; I will take the heart of stone out of your flesh and give you a heart of flesh."* As Holy Spirit led, we shared prophetic utterances with one another, building each other up in faith and love.

Returning to daily life, I had the opportunity to minister at a men's prison. During this visit, the Lord allowed me to speak a prophetic word that encouraged the men at a trustee camp to stay the course and trust the process. I reminded them of the truth found in *Proverbs* 16:9 (NKJV): *"A man's heart plans his way, but the Lord directs his steps."* I shared how we serve an "outside-the-box" God who is fully aware of everything happening outside of our control. The men learned that where they were at that moment was not their final destination—God had a plan to prosper them and give them hope.

The outcome of that service was extraordinary. One man gave his life to Christ, and after his release, he was reunited with his wife. During their reunion, he shared with her the story of how Holy Spirit used Henri Williams to minister to him in prison. In a divine twist, the wife he reconnected with was one of the new Sisters I had met at the spiritual retreat hosted by my spiritual mom—the very retreat where my sister Gloria had flown into Houston to join us.

This testimony serves as a reminder of how intricately God weaves our lives together for His glory. He uses the connections we make and the words we speak, in both large and small ways, to demonstrate His love and sovereignty.

GIVING MONEY TO A MAN – MARCH 2011

One morning on my way to work, Holy Spirit instructed me not to drive down I-10. Despite this, my human reasoning convinced me that I knew a shortcut, and I proceeded as planned. Along the way, I stopped for gas on Weslayan off I-59 near Lakewood Church. At the corner,

Call for The Prophetic Intercessor

I noticed a man dressed in a three-piece suit, and Holy Spirit said, "Give him $20."

I hesitated. Giving money to a man went against my personal principles. Instead, I went into the gas station, bought a honey bun, a strawberry lemonade Snapple, and paid for my gas. As I placed the remaining cash in my cup holder, I heard Holy Spirit's voice again, urging me to give the man $20. I wrestled internally, standing there with my hand on the gas pump, until I heard His voice a third time, now with unmistakable insistence: "I told you to give that man $20."

I finally relented. I retrieved the $20 from my cup holder and walked over to the man. Tapping him on the arm, I said, "Sir," and handed him the money. His reaction stunned me. Tears streamed down his face as he explained, "The Lord told me to come here and wait, and I was obedient. My wife and I just moved into apartments down the street, and our car broke down. I have a new job starting today, and I didn't want to leave her, but she insisted. I will use this money to catch a cab to work and have already asked for an advance on my paycheck to fix the car."

Driving away, I wept as the Lord spoke to my heart: "I'm teaching you obedience, Daughter." Yet, even after experiencing the sweetness of God's confirmation, I reverted to

Call for The Prophetic Intercessor

my own understanding. I turned onto I-10, ignoring His earlier instruction. Running late due to my earlier hesitation, I thought my shortcut would save time. However, I encountered three police cars that slowed me down further, each one a reminder of my disobedience.

At a stoplight, I saw a homeless man on the corner, and Holy Spirit prompted me to give him the leftovers from a Pontchartrain dinner I had saved for lunch. I ignored Him and drove through the light. God's voice came again: "Go back, and now give him your lunch, the $5 in your cup holder, your honey bun, and the Snapple." Frustrated, I grudgingly complied, throwing everything into a bag and handing it to the man. His gratitude contrasted starkly with my attitude. As I sped away, God convicted me: "I'm after THAT attitude, Daughter."

By the time I arrived at work, my mood was foul. I knew my attitude wouldn't glorify God, so I closed my office door to avoid interacting with anyone. Shortly after, an intercom call summoned all managers to a meeting. Still grumbling internally, I sarcastically told God, "I guess I'm on a supernatural fast today."

At the meeting, our Regional Director announced, "I'm taking the entire staff to lunch at Pappadeaux's. Order anything you want, including dessert." In that moment, I realized God had been preparing me for a blessing. The meal I begrudgingly gave away was replaced with something better, reminding me of 1 Samuel 9:23-24 (NIV): "*Samuel said to the cook, 'Bring the piece of meat I gave you, the one I told you to lay aside.' So, the cook took up the thigh with what was on it and set it in front of Saul. Samuel said, 'Here is what has been kept for you. Eat, because it was set aside for you for this occasion.'*"

This experience taught me that God was addressing the selfishness still lingering in my heart. He used these moments to refine me, burning off impurities and teaching me complete dependence on Him. Through the conviction of 2 *Timothy* 3:16 (KJV)— "*All scripture is given by inspiration of God, and is profitable for doctrine, for reproof, for correction, for instruction in righteousness*"— I realized the necessity of immediate and joyful obedience.

God used these situations to teach both the man in the suit and me to trust His voice. I learned that obedience to God requires faith, humility, and a willingness to let go of my own desires. From this experience, I now strive to respond to His voice with greater immediacy, understanding that His plans are always better than my own.

Call for The Prophetic Intercessor

GO BACK AND GET WHAT YOU LEFT BEHIND – OCTOBER 2024

Recently, I was invited to participate in a board retreat for a ministry called Healed in Mercy. After praying, I felt that this was something the Lord wanted me to do. This ministry aligns deeply with how the Lord operates through me, as I pray that mercy, compassion, and healing are always components of what people experience when God ministers through me.

The retreat was set in Tow, Texas, and the night before, I was up late working on this manuscript. By 3:00 a.m., I still hadn't packed, and my house was in total disarray as I was also preparing for my spiritual daughter's annual retreat the following weekend. Bags, packages, and papers were scattered in every room, creating an atmosphere of confusion around me.

My plan was to attend an 8:30 a.m. chapel service before heading out, but I remembered I needed to pick up a prescription from the pharmacy, which didn't open until 8:00 a.m. This meant missing chapel. When I arrived at the pharmacy, the prescription wasn't ready, and the pharmacist asked me to return in 20 minutes. Frustrated, I went back home.

Call for The Prophetic Intercessor

Walking in, I was greeted by my alarm blaring and the refrigerator door wide open. As I turned off the alarm and closed the fridge, Holy Spirit spoke: "If you hadn't come back, the alarm would have been going off all weekend, and your food would have spoiled."

I returned to the pharmacy only to wait another 20 minutes for the prescription. By then, my plans for the morning were slipping away. I realized I had made my own checklist for the day without consulting God about His plans for me.

With the prescription finally in hand, I went to Walmart for gas, only to remember I didn't have my credit cards. Both my debit and credit accounts had been hacked the week before, and I hadn't adjusted to carrying cash. Feeling uneasy about traveling with cash, I returned home to retrieve it.

At home, I noticed my phone charger hanging on the laundry room doorknob. Holy Spirit reminded me of a previous trip when my phone had refused to charge, causing unnecessary stress. Grateful for the reminder, I packed the charger and prepared to leave again.

Before leaving, Holy Spirit prompted me to take my large print Bible. He said, "I want you to start turning the pages of your physical Bible again. When I speak to you and download revelations, write them in the margins." Searching the house for the Bible, I couldn't find it, and as I headed out the door again, Holy Spirit reminded me: "You forgot to pack underwear and pajamas!" I packed what I needed and left for the third time.

As I finally drove away, I glanced into the back seat and saw my large Bible already there. Relieved, I continued on, stopping at the community mailbox. Inside, I found a new credit card from Chase Bank. I wept, realizing that God had orchestrated everything to ensure I could travel safely without anxiety.

Turning the corner to leave my subdivision, Holy Spirit prompted me to return home for the fourth time. This time, I found my appointment book and the papers I needed for the trip, sitting in plain view in the garage. At that moment, Holy Spirit said, "Call the visionary of Healed in Mercy and tell her you're not traveling today. You're exhausted, and if you get on the road, you'll be in a car accident. I'm taking you back, Daughter, to pick up things you've left behind, to close doors, and to remind you of promises I still intend to keep in your life."

Obediently, I made the call. The Lord revealed to me how my exhaustion and self-reliance had caused me to overlook His guidance. Through this experience, I was reminded of

His love and protection, as well as the importance of resting in Him and seeking His plans over my own.

I'm so grateful to know His voice and to follow in obedience, even when it disrupts my plans. God used this situation to show me that He is always working to prepare and protect me, and that trusting Him fully is the only way to walk in His perfect will.

MOBILE MECHANIC – NOVEMBER 2024

On November 13, 2024, while out running errands, my car battery died, leading me to return the battery to Walmart for an exchange. As I worked with the technician to swap the faulty battery and replace the loaned one, we began to talk. During our conversation, I felt the Lord impress upon me to tell him that he needed to start his own business. Obediently, I shared what I heard and encouraged him to consider starting a mobile mechanic shop specifically marketed to single women.

I told him that I knew many single women who desperately needed a trustworthy mechanic—someone integral, who wouldn't take advantage of them. His reaction confirmed the divine timing of the moment. He shared that he had just been talking to his coworkers about leaving Walmart to start his own business. His plan was to use his upcoming tax return to fund the venture.

Our conversation deepened as he revealed he was a Christian. I felt led to give him my pastor's phone number and invited him to the Tuesday night men's group at my church. I also encouraged him to contact me when he got his business up and running so I could make referrals for him.

Looking back, I believe Holy Spirit orchestrated this encounter. He led me to that particular Walmart, connected me with the right person, and gave me the words to encourage and empower this young man. It was a reminder of how God uses seemingly ordinary moments to promote Kingdom outcomes, lifting others up and advancing His plans through obedience and connection.

FINAL WORDS

Do you believe that God has called you to be a prophetic intercessor? Intercessory prayer, at its core, is praying on behalf of others, but when combined with a prophetic gift, it becomes a transformative partnership with God. This type of prayer invites us into a deeper relationship with Him, where we discern His heart, align with His will, and pray His plans into reality.

Prophetic intercession challenges us to seek God in everything we do, glorifying Him and reflecting Christ in our daily walk. It goes beyond presenting our own desires or petitions and instead focuses on actively listening for God's voice and praying in agreement with His revealed purposes. This unique dimension of intercession requires a sensitivity to Holy Spirit, a willingness to stand in the gap for others, and a commitment to align our prayers with God's will.

The role of a prophetic intercessor is not only to pray for others but to serve as a vessel for God's truth and plans. As seen in Scriptures such as 1 Timothy 2:1-6 and Psalm 5:3 (NKJV)—

Call for The Prophetic Intercessor

"My voice You shall hear in the morning, O Lord; In the morning I will direct it to You, and I will look up"—a prophetic intercessor's posture is one of seeking, listening, and obeying. Through this posture, we partner with God to bring about His purposes on earth.

Ultimately, prophetic intercession is about stepping into the flow of God's Spirit, listening for His guidance, and praying with faith and boldness. It is a sacred calling that requires obedience, humility, and a heart surrendered to His will. If you feel the stirring of this call in your spirit, be encouraged. God equips those He calls, and as you grow in your relationship with Him, He will reveal His plans and guide you into this powerful ministry of prayer. May you embrace the privilege of being a prophetic intercessor, standing in the gap and partnering with the Lord to bring His will to fruition in the lives of others.

A CALL TO ACTION

To step into your calling as a prophetic intercessor, it is essential to align your life with God's principles and directives. Your prophetic alignment begins here:

1. **Put God First.** Prioritize seeking God's Kingdom and righteousness in your daily walk, trusting that He will provide all that is necessary for your calling. As Jesus taught:

> "Seek the Kingdom of God above all else, and live righteously, and He will give you everything you need," Matthew 6:33 (NLT).

2. **Seek the Face of God.** We are commanded to humble ourselves and seek Him. Develop an earnest desire to know God and pursue Him with humility and repentance.

> "And My people, who are called by My Name, humble themselves, and pray and seek (crave, require as a necessity) My face and turn from their wicked ways, then I will hear [them] from heaven, and forgive their sin and heal their land. Now My eyes will be open and My

Call for The Prophetic Intercessor

ears attentive to prayer offered in this place",
2 Chronicles 7:14-15 (AMP).

3. **Read His Word.** Reading and meditating on God's Word lays the foundation for hearing from Him. Scripture is the basis of all prophetic intercession, providing guidance, truth, and direction.

"This Book of the Law shall not depart from your mouth, but you shall read [and meditate on] it day and night, so that you may be careful to do [everything] in accordance with all that is written in it; for then you will make your way prosperous, and then you will be successful",
Joshua 1:8 (AMP).

4. **Posture Your Heart.** Allow God to circumcise your heart, removing anything that hinders intimacy with Him. Position yourself to receive His instructions with a heart surrendered to His will.

"Behold, the heavens and the highest of heavens belong to the Lord your God, the earth and all that is in it. Yet the Lord had a delight in loving your fathers and set His affection on them, and He chose their descendants after them, you above all peoples, as it is this day. So, circumcise

[that is, remove sin from] your heart, and be stiff-necked (stubborn, obstinate) no longer. For the Lord your God is the God of gods and the Lord of lords, the great, the mighty, the awesome God who does not show partiality nor take a bribe", Deuteronomy 10:14-17 (AMP).

5. **Learn to Recognize His Voice.** Spend intentional time in prayer, worship, and His Word to distinguish His voice from your own thoughts or external distractions. As Jesus said:

"My sheep listen to my voice; I know them, and they follow me", John 10:27 (NIV).

6. **Be Obedient.** Follow His instructions promptly and completely. Obedience opens the door for greater intimacy and clarity in your prophetic journey.

"Samuel said, 'Has the Lord as great a delight in burnt offerings and sacrifices. As in obedience to the voice of the Lord? Behold, to obey is better than sacrifice, and to heed [is better] than the fat of rams'", 1 Samuel 15:22 (AMP).

7. **Speak Only What God Reveals.** Resist the temptation to add or take away from what

Call for The Prophetic Intercessor

God has shown you. Faithfully declare His words, trusting His timing and wisdom.

"For prophecy never had its origin in the human will, but prophets, though human, spoke from God as they were carried along by Holy Spirit." 2 Peter 1:21 (NIV)

8. **Pray for His Kingdom to Come.** Model your prayers after Jesus' example:

"May your Kingdom come soon. May your will be done on earth, as it is in heaven." Matthew 6:10 (NLT).

Align your intercession with His will, asking for His Kingdom to manifest in the lives and situations you pray over.

By following these steps, you position yourself for prophetic alignment with God's will. Trust Him to guide you, equip you, and use you as a vessel for His purposes. Begin today by seeking His face, listening for His voice, and stepping into the transformative power of prophetic intercession.

Call for The Prophetic Intercessor

A PRAYER FOR YOU

Heavenly Father,
We come before You with hearts open and surrendered, seeking Your guidance and wisdom. Thank You for calling Your children to the ministry of prophetic intercession, for entrusting them with the privilege of standing in the gap for others. Lord, we acknowledge that this calling is not by our might or power, but by Your Spirit.

Father, I lift up every reader who feels the stirring of Your Spirit within them, drawing them closer to this sacred ministry. Strengthen their faith and deepen their understanding of Your will. Teach them to hear Your voice clearly, to discern Your heart, and to pray with power and precision according to Your purposes.

Circumcise their hearts, Lord, removing anything that would hinder their intimacy with You. Fill them with Your Spirit, equipping them to walk in obedience, humility, and boldness. Teach them to seek Your face daily and to align their prayers with heaven's agenda.

We pray that You will guide them as they grow in this ministry, giving them wisdom, revelation, and discernment. Help them to intercede with compassion, patience, and unwavering faith. Let their words be seasoned

Call for The Prophetic Intercessor

with grace and truth, bringing healing, restoration, and transformation to those they lift up in prayer.
Father, just as Jesus intercedes for us at Your right hand, empower these prophetic intercessors to reflect His heart in their prayers. May they be vessels through which Your Kingdom comes, and Your will is done on earth as it is in heaven.
We ask for Your protection over their minds, hearts, and spirits as they step into this calling. Surround them with Your peace, guard them with Your truth, and guide them with Your light. May they always rely on Your strength and never grow weary in doing good.
Lord, we thank You for their willingness to answer this call. Bless them abundantly as they partner with You in prayer. Let their ministry bear fruit that glorifies Your name and advances Your Kingdom.
In Jesus' mighty and matchless name, we pray, Amen.

ABOUT THE CONTRIBUTOR

Dr. Henri Williams, known as Dr. Henri, is a dedicated minister with over 25 years of experience. She is a sought-after speaker, preacher, teacher, and mentor, recognized for

Call for The Prophetic Intercessor

her clear and impactful delivery of the Word. Dr. Henri has traveled internationally, ministering at women's conferences and retreats, and offering pastoral and leadership training. She holds a double major in Psychology and Sociology, along with advanced degrees in Theology and Christian Counseling. Currently, she serves as the Chaplain and Spiritual Life Coordinator at a 600-bed homeless shelter in Houston and is an active member of The Fellowship of Purpose Church, led by Sr. Pastor Byron and Lady Marcella Murray.

ADDITIONAL BOOKS FROM THE EDITOR

Let The Church Grieve: After reading Let The Church Grieve the reader will be able to understand and acknowledge that grief is the inevitable process that human beings will experience as the result of a loss at some point in their lives and the journey of grief demands the attention of the local church and spiritual communities.  The reader will also be equipped with the basic knowledge and tools needed to educate others within their spiritual communities on what grief is, what support looks like, and how to start a grief support group within their spiritual communities, allowing the congregation to provide permission, time, and space to support those who are grieving.

Let The Church Grieve Companion Workbook: Let The Church Grieve: An Interactive Workbook is your companion through this difficult time, offering practical exercises, reflective journal prompts, and

spiritual guidance to help you and your community navigate the complex emotions of loss.

Close The Door: This book is not just another book on prayer. Close The Door is a book that teaches the reader the importance of building an intimate relationship with God in prayer, behind Closed Door based on The Lord's Prayer taken from Matthew 6.

Open Wide Your Mouth: Opening our mouth is about spending time with God in our places of vulnerability, our place of privacy, our place of comfortability where we are seen and experienced for who we really are without all the frills.

The Scandalous Love of God: This book will open your eyes to see the ways that God has, is, and will continue to solidify His love for you. You will see, too, what scandalous extremes God will go to just to get you to understand the depths of His love for you.

Begin Again: There are things in life that happen, and they are not always in our control. Things like the downfall of the economy, natural disasters, the loss of a loved one, a home, a marriage, a business, or a job to name a few, but the good news is that it's never too late to "BEGIN AGAIN".  Believe it or not, beginning again happens every second of the day for someone around the world. Despite what you may tell yourself or what others may say, it's never too late to "BEGIN AGAIN" where you left off.

Begin Again Workbook and Monthly Planner: Unlock your potential and embrace the journey of transformation with the Begin Again Workbook and Monthly Planner. This powerful resource is designed to guide you through the process of self-discovery, helping you set meaningful goals and develop actionable plans to bring your dreams to life.

Aurora's Grief Journey: When Aurora loses her beloved grandfather, she is overwhelmed by sadness, anger, and confusion. Guided by her family's love

and faith, she begins to understand that it's okay to feel all these emotions. From struggling with anger at God to finding comfort in prayer, Aurora's journey highlights the importance of sharing feelings, honoring precious memories, and leaning on loved ones.

Asa's Big Day Out: A Dinosaur Adventure and a Journey of Bravery: Asa loves dinosaurs but struggles with social anxiety, making crowded places challenging. When his mom and Aunt take him and Kash to a dinosaur exhibition, Asa learns that bravery isn't about being fearless—it's about expressing how you feel and taking small steps forward.

www.ingramcontent.com/pod-product-compliance
Lightning Source LLC
Chambersburg PA
CBHW022049160426
43198CB00008B/172